frontline history

Cold War

1945 – 1991

Derrick Murphy

SERIES EDITOR DERRICK MURPHY

Published by Collins Educational
An imprint of HarperCollins*Publishers* Ltd
77–85 Fulham Palace Road
Hammersmith
London
W6 8JB

www.**Collins**Education.com
On-line support for schools and colleges

ISBN 0 00 715504 2

British Library Cataloguing in Publication Data.
A catalogue record for this publication is available from the British Library.

Edited by Will Chuter
Design by Sally Boothroyd
Cover design by BarkerHilsdon
Picture research by Celia Dearing
Artwork by Richard Morris
Production by Sarah Robinson
Index compiled by Julie Rimington
Printed and bound by Printing Express Ltd, Hong Kong

Contents

Using your factual knowledge of the Cold War from 1945 to 1991 effectively is very important to success in this area of GCSE Modern World History. This book is designed to provide the essential information. It contains:

• The important questions asked at GCSE
• Detailed information about key historical events and characters
• Written and visual sources
• Differing historical interpretations about the period you are studying

This Study Skills section is designed to help you do your best at GCSE Modern World History. Many of the skills are developments from what you covered in Key Stage 3 History:

• How to explain and use written sources
• How to evaluate cartoons, photographs, maps and graphs
• How to develop extended writing

When you are studying the individual topics in this book make sure that you refer back to these pages for guidance.

HOW TO EXPLAIN AND USE WRITTEN SOURCES

You may have learnt at Key Stage 3 that there are two types of sources: primary and secondary. Primary sources are either produced at the time of the event or produced after the event by a witness of the event. Secondary sources are those written after the event by someone who did not witness the event. Although knowing whether a source is primary or secondary is important, it is more important to explain whether it is **useful** or **reliable**.

What does a source show?
Sometimes you are asked to explain what a source reveals about a particular subject. **Remember: always look at the precise wording of a question.** The question may only ask you to explain certain parts of the source.

EXAMPLE 1 – look at Source 2, p45

Question What does this source reveal about the attitude of the North Vietnamese Army towards fighting the American War in Vietnam?
In your answer, you need to mention that the North Vietnamese general, Giap, aimed to wear down the American forces in South Vietnam, rather than force them out of the country. The source also says that this tactic was adopted for a specific reason: the North Vietnamese Army was not strong enough to push them out forcefully. You do not need to use your own knowledge or any other source material in answering this question

How reliable is a source?
A reliable source is one that contains an accurate or objective view of a past event. Because different people see past events from different viewpoints, it is difficult for any source to be completely reliable. **Be careful: both primary sources and secondary sources may be unreliable.**

What makes a source unreliable?
A source may be unreliable because it contains **bias**. This means that the person producing the source may wish to look at a past event from a particular viewpoint. The person might have a **motive** for producing the source in a particular way.

EXAMPLE 2 – look at Source 3, p15

Question How reliable is this source as evidence of why the Marshall Plan was introduced?
Ask yourself these questions:

• *Did the person writing the source have a motive for being biased?*
Yes. The person who produced the source was the Soviet Deputy Foreign Minister. Therefore, his views were likely to be anti-American. He was also speaking at the United Nations, which might mean that he was trying to persuade other countries to agree with his point of view. He was making a public statement showing the USSR's opposition to the Marshall Plan.

• *Does the source contain **objective** or **subjective** information?*
Objective information means factual information. Subjective information means someone's opinion. If a source contains a lot of subjective information, it is likely to be **biased**. This source contains both objective and subjective information.
Objective information: "It is a plan to create a bloc of countries…"
Subjective information: "This Plan is an attempt to split Europe into two camps…[it is] hostile to the USSR."

Even though a source may contain a lot of facts (objective information) it may still be unreliable. **You will need to test the information against your own knowledge or other sources.**

Some of the information in the source is true. However, the source doesn't mention that the USA offered Marshall Aid to the USSR and all the countries of Eastern Europe, and that the USSR refused to accept it.

How useful is a source?

To answer this question correctly, you need to think about exactly whom it's useful to. Usually this appears in the question, e.g. 'How useful is this source to an historian writing about…?'

To decide how useful a source might be, you need to look at its strengths, then list them. Then decide what the source's limitations are - what it doesn't mention - then list them. Once you have done this look at your lists. Does the source contain more strengths than weaknesses? If so, you could say that the source is quite useful.

EXAMPLE 3 – look at Source 1, p18

Question How useful is this source as evidence of why NATO was created in 1949?

List of strengths
• The source is part of the original treaty.
• It contains information on what NATO hoped to achieve. In Article 1, this was to solve international disputes by peaceful means. In Article 5, this was the idea of mutual self-defence. An attack on one member was regarded as an attack on all members.

List of limitations
• It contains only two parts of the Treaty.
• The source only contains basic information about NATO. It doesn't state that the Treaty was created immediately after the Berlin Airlift crisis of 1948-1949.
• It doesn't mention that a cold war had developed between the USA and its allies, and the USSR, and that this was one of the reasons behind NATO's creation

The source contains only a limited amount of information. You need to **test this information against your own knowledge to decide how useful it is.**

HOW TO EVALUATE VISUAL SOURCES

Cartoons, photographs, posters, graphs, and maps are all different types of visual sources. **As with written sources, you also need to test the usefulness and reliability of visual sources.**

Cartoons

Cartoons are usually produced to convey a political **message** or **statement**. Cartoons are used because they can give an immediate, visual message in a way that a written source cannot.

EXAMPLE 4 – look at Source 3, p35

This is a cartoon produced in Britain during the Cuban Missile crisis of 1962. It shows US President Kennedy and Soviet Premier Khrushchev sitting on H-bombs, arm wrestling.

The cartoon is making a political point, so there is a **motive** for showing the two leaders in this way. The cartoon is trying to show that the Cuban Missile crisis was extremely serious. It shows the two leaders – representatives of their countries – struggling with each other. It suggests that the struggle is so serious that they might end up using nuclear weapons to resolve it.

Using your own knowledge of the period you will know that the Cuban Missile crisis was the most serious series of events in the entire Cold War. It was feared that both sides might use nuclear weapons, plunging the world into nuclear war and destruction. The crisis only ended when Soviet Premier Khrushchev agreed to remove Soviet missiles from Cuba, after Kennedy's blockade of the island.

Photographs

'The camera never lies!' This is a commonly used phrase that is not necessarily true. Sometimes a picture does not tell the whole story. Therefore, you need to **test** the photograph by providing **corroborative** evidence. This means using your own knowledge or referring to other sources.

EXAMPLE 5 – look at Source 1, p27

Question How useful is this photograph as evidence of the fighting during the Hungarian Uprising of 1956?
This photograph shows a Hungarian tank passing a burnt-out Soviet tank in Budapest during the uprising of 1956.

However, to **test** whether this photograph reflects what happened during the Hungarian Uprising, you need to provide **corroborative evidence**. This means using your own knowledge or referring to other sources.

You will know that, in the early stages of the uprising, the Hungarian rebels took over the capital, Budapest. However, within a week, the Soviet Red Army had recaptured the city. So, this photograph might be useful in showing what took place in the early part of the uprising. However, it gives a false overall view of the uprising because the USSR was able the crush it within a week.

Posters

Posters are usually produced for a particular reason. They tend to serve the purposes of the person who has paid for them to be made. These people have **motives** for presenting the poster in a particular way.

EXAMPLE 6 – look at Source 2, p15

Question How does this poster promote the Marshall Plan?
This poster has either been produced by Germans who support the Marshall Plan, or Americans. It is aimed at the German people. Its motive is to encourage Germans to view the Marshall Plan in a positive light. It does this by using the image of a truck entering Germany, covered in the flags of the other nations who will receive Plan aid. The truck is meant to be American, carrying food and other aid, and the badge on its bonnet reads 'ERP' – 'European Recovery Plan'. The truck sails through German customs ('*zoll*') on a free road ('*freie bahn*'), signifying that it is allowed and welcomed in Germany. This is particularly relevant since, only three years before, Germany had been at war with the USA. It shows that Marshall Aid is being introduced to help Germany. This contrasts with the way the Soviets viewed the Marshall Plan – look at Source 3, p15.

Graphs, maps and statistical data

Graphs, maps and statistical data are sometimes used to help students understand information more easily than providing a written source.

EXAMPLE 7 – look at Source 3, p13

This graph shows the difference in support for communist parties across Eastern Europe before and after 1946. It also shows how that support differed from country to country. Statistical data gives you precise information. Here it allows you to see the dramatic change of communist support in a way a written source might not. It provides instant confirmation of the effect of the Soviet clampdown on Eastern European governments after 1946.

EXAMPLE 8 – look at Source 3, p25

This diagram shows the growth of Soviet and US nuclear weapons production in the 1960s. It provides information about how serious the arms race was in a way that a written source might not. Statistical information like this can also show **trends** – how each superpower reacted to the other's weapons production over the decade. However, statistical data can have limitations. Although this diagram shows the balance of weapons, it doesn't show where they were deployed.

EXAMPLE 9 – look at Source 2, p11

Maps have a similar value in presenting information in a way a written source cannot. This map shows the division of Europe after the Yalta and Potsdam conferences.

It allows you to see exactly how much territory Germany lost at the end of the Second World War, and the exact location of it. It also shows the way in which Germany, Austria, and Berlin were divided into four military zones of occupation after the war.

HOW TO ANSWER EXTENDED WRITING QUESTIONS

These questions require a detailed factual answer. Knowing the information contained in this book is extremely important. To make sure that you use the information correctly you need to:

- **Make sure you answer the question on the paper.** It's a bad idea to write an answer for a question that is not on the paper just because you have prepared for it!

- **Make a short plan for your intended question.** This should show the order you want to set out the information in your answer. It will also help ensure you don't leave out important information whilst writing your answer.

- **Write in paragraphs.** Each paragraph should contain an important point you wish to make.

- **Remember important dates.** Or try to remember the sequence of events.

- **Use historical terms** (e.g. superpower, communist, capitalist, Mutually Assured Destruction – M.A.D., détente, guerrilla warfare) **correctly**. **Also use key words** (e.g. pact, treaty, alliance, plan) **correctly**.

- **Understand the role of important individuals** (e.g. US Presidents Truman, Kennedy, Nixon, and Reagan; Soviet Premiers Stalin, Khrushchev, Brezhnev, and Gorbachev; Alexander Dubcek and Lech Walesa).

- **Make sure you spell historical words correctly.** You must also try to use good punctuation and grammar. Poor 'SPG' can cost you marks.

- **Try to make links between various paragraphs.** If you are asked to explain why the Cold War began from 1945, it is important to link the causes you identify. They could be:

> **Long Term Cause** US fear of communism since the communist Revolution of 1917 in Russia; Soviet fear of the capitalist West.
>
> **Short Term Causes** Mutual suspicion during the Yalta and Potsdam conferences in 1945.
>
> **Immediate Cause** The Soviet takeover of Eastern Europe; Churchill's Iron Curtain speech; the Truman Doctrine and Marshall Aid.

Or you could mention causes in order of importance. If you do this, give an explanation for putting them in that order.

- **Write a brief conclusion.** This could just be one sentence at the end. But it is essential because it contains your **judgement**. In the question above, what would you regard as the **most important** reason behind the start of the Cold War?

HOW THIS BOOK MATCHES THE EXAM SPECIFICATIONS

Chapters in this book	AQA, History B, Paper 1, Section A, Option X	Edexcel History A, Papers 1 and 2	OCR History B: core content
1 THE ORIGINS OF THE COLD WAR	Key Issue 7	Paper 1, Section A: A6	Key Question 4
2 THE DEVELOPMENT OF THE COLD WAR	Key Issue 8	Paper 1, Section A: A6	Key Question 6
3 THE CUBAN MISSILE CRISIS, 1962 – A CASE STUDY	Key Issue 9	Paper 1, Section A: A6	Key Question 5
4 THE VIETNAM WAR	Key Issue 10	Paper 2, Section B: B7	Key Question 5
5 PRAGUE, CHINA, AND DÉTENTE	Key Issue 10 Key Issue 11	Paper 1, Section A: A6	Key Question 6
6 THE NEW COLD WAR, 1979-85	Key Issue 12	Paper 1, Section A: A6	Key Question 6
7 THE END OF THE COLD WAR, 1985-91	Key Issue 13	Paper 1, Section A: A6	Key Question 6

What was the Cold War?

The Cold War was a conflict between the USA and its allies, and the USSR (Union of Soviet Socialist Republics) and its allies. It lasted from the end of the Second World War in 1945 until the fall of the USSR in 1991. It did not involve any direct fighting between the two countries. It was, instead, a sustained period of international tension. This helps distinguish the Cold War from a 'hot war', which would have involved direct combat between the two sides.

The USA and USSR were the two most dominant powers in the world between 1945 and 1991. They were known as the 'superpowers' because of their immense military strength. They were also the two largest economies in the world during this period.

So, if the Cold War did not involve any actual fighting between the USA and USSR, what did take place?

WHAT ACTUALLY HAPPENED IN THE COLD WAR?

Armed forces on constant alert

Both the USA and USSR kept large armed forces on almost constant war alert. Each side was prepared for an attack by the other. They both had extensive early warning systems. From the late 1940s to 1991, it seemed that they were always on the verge of outright war.

Spying and surveillance

Both the USA and the USSR used spying and surveillance to check on the other's activities. Initially, spies from each side entered enemy territory and reported back on the other. Later, special aircraft were used. Finally, a large system of spy satellites was set up by both sides to monitor each other. The main US spy organisation was the CIA (Central Intelligence Agency). The main Soviet spy agency was the KGB (part of the Soviet Security Service).

Nuclear, chemical and biological weapons

Both the USA and USSR possessed nuclear weapons from 1949. As the conflict developed, a possible war between them also meant that the whole world might be destroyed in an all-out nuclear war. By 1991 both sides possessed thousands of nuclear weapons and extensive stocks of chemical and biological weapons. This turned the Cold War into something that affected the whole world.

Conflicting political ideals

The Cold War was incredibly tense because each side believed that the other wanted to dominate the world with their political ideals.

Soviet communism

The USA saw the USSR as the centre of communism. Americans believed that the Soviets wanted to make the whole world communist. This had been the aim of the USSR's first leader, Lenin, in the early 1920s. The USSR was the only country in the world without a geographical limitation in its name. The USA believed that the communist plan was to make the whole world Soviet Socialist Republics.

> **communism**
> *the belief that all property and means of production should be shared by the community or state*

American capitalism

The USSR thought the USA wanted to make the whole world into one large capitalist economy. They feared that the USA would dominate this. In a capitalist economy there was also a wide gap between the very rich and the very poor. The USSR saw itself as trying to create a socialist society. In this type of society there would be only a small difference between rich and poor.

> **capitalism**
> *economic system in which property and industry is privately owned*

Trade restrictions

In order to protect itself against US economic influence, the USSR prevented direct trade with America and the West. Eastern Europe and other communist-controlled areas were forced to trade only with the USSR and each other. As a result, there seemed to be a very obvious division between communist and non-communist areas during the Cold War. These became known as blocs.

> **bloc**
> *people or countries combined by a common interest, in this case Soviet communism and US-led capitalism*

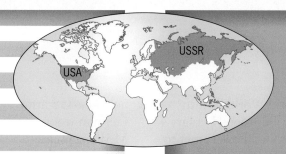

- A democracy with free elections
- An economy and society based on the private ownership of business and homes
- The USA was mainly Christian and feared 'godless communism'
- The USA believed the USSR was trying to make the whole world communist

- A one-party dictatorship run by the Communist Party
- An economy based on state control. The Soviet government owned all business and homes
- The Soviet government was atheistic (did not believe in a God)
- The Soviet government believed the USA wanted to destroy communism

The USA and the USSR in 1945 compared.

Active fighting in other parts of the world

Because both the USA and the USSR saw their type of society as the model for other countries, the Cold War involved conflict in other parts of the world. Latin America, the Middle East, Asia and Africa were all affected by the struggle between the two superpowers. Occasionally, it led to actual fighting. The USA sent troops to fight North Korea – an ally of the USSR – in the Korean War (1950-1953). The USA also sent troops to South Vietnam in the Vietnam War (1965-1973) to stop it from becoming communist. Both powers tried to influence governments across the globe with their points of view.

A HISTORY OF TENSION

To many historians, the Cold War began once Germany and Japan had been defeated at the end of the Second World War. Yet tension between these two countries can be traced back to the Communist Revolution in Russia in October 1917. When the Communist Party took control of Russia in 1917, they claimed that they wanted to spread communism across the globe. From that time the USA feared Russia and communism.

FREEZES AND THAWS

During the Cold War, relations between the USA and the USSR were not constant. Sometimes they seemed on the brink of war. These periods were called 'freezes' because they represented a cooling of relations between the two powers.

At other times attempts were made to encourage better relations. These were called 'thaws'.

The Cuban Missile crisis of October 1962 was the most serious freeze. It was the nearest both sides came to all-out nuclear war. From 1972 to 1979 the two countries tried to reduce tension. This was the period of détente.

détente
joint effort by the superpowers to improve US-Soviet relations

Questions

1. Explain the meaning of these Cold War terms:
   a) communist
   b) superpower
   c) freeze and thaw
2. Why weren't the USA and the USSR on friendly terms between 1917 and 1941? Give reasons for your answer.
3. 'The rivalry between the USA and the USSR during the Cold War was because each superpower feared the other.' Do you agree with this statement? Use information in this section to explain your answer.

The Yalta and Potsdam Conferences, 1945

By February 1945 the Second World War in Europe was nearing its end. Between February 4 and 12, the leaders of the Allied Powers met to discuss the post-war world. Three countries were dominant: the USA, the USSR and Britain. They met in Yalta, in the USSR.

THE 'BIG THREE' AT YALTA

SOURCE 1

Winston Churchill, Franklin D. Roosevelt and Josef Stalin at Yalta.

Josef Stalin

Stalin had been dictator of the USSR since 1924. He had transformed the country into a major industrial economy and one of the world's strongest military powers. During the Second World War the Soviet army did more than any other to defeat Nazi Germany. Over 20 million Soviet citizens died in the war, including 13 million members of the armed forces. By comparison, Britain had lost only 300,000 and the USA 500,000. However, by February 1945 the USSR had the largest army in the world. This army – the Red Army – was preparing to attack Berlin, Germany's capital.

Franklin D. Roosevelt (FDR)

FDR had been leader of the USA since 1933. The longest-serving President in US history, he had helped the USA out of the economic depression of the early 1930s. He was also very influential in involving the USA in the war in Europe. But FDR only survived the Yalta Conference by two months, dying in April 1945. By early 1945 the USA was the world's greatest economic power. It supplied war materials and food to all its allies, including the USSR. It possessed the world's largest navy and

air force. US armed forces had helped defeat German troops in Western Europe and the Mediterranean. The USA was also on the verge of defeating Japan. Unbeknownst to the USSR at the time of the Yalta Conference, the USA was developing a nuclear weapon.

Winston Churchill

Churchill was Prime Minister of the United Kingdom and representative of the British Empire. British troops had fought Nazi Germany longer than the USA or the USSR but, by 1945, Britain was almost bankrupt. It kept fighting because it received aid from the USA. During the war Britain lost its position as the world's greatest naval power. By February 1945 Britain was much less powerful than either the USSR or the USA.

THE YALTA CONFERENCE

What was decided at Yalta?

How to defeat Hitler and Japan
The Red Army would take Berlin, Vienna and Prague, securing the defeat of the Nazis. Stalin also agreed to join the war against Japan within three months of the end of the war against Germany.

Zones of occupation in Germany, Austria, Berlin and Vienna
Once Germany and Austria were defeated, they would be occupied by the Allied armies. They would then be divided into four military zones, controlled by the USA, the USSR, Britain, and France. Although Berlin and Vienna were to be within the Soviet zone of occupation, these two cities were also divided into four military zones.

Free elections in Poland and Eastern Europe
Poland was occupied by the Red Army, and a government of Polish communists had been set up. This was a major concern because Britain had gone to war in 1939 to keep Poland free of Hitler's dictatorship, and now it seemed it might fall under Stalin's. However, Stalin promised free and fair elections in Poland and the rest of Soviet-occupied Eastern Europe.

Polish territorial changes
Stalin also wanted back Soviet territory given to Poland in 1921. This meant Poland lost

nearly 30 per cent of its land. In return, Poland was given a large part of eastern Germany.

The United Nations

The USSR agreed to the new United Nations being based in New York City. It approved France as a permanent member of the UN Security Council, along with the USA, USSR and Britain.

THE POTSDAM CONFERENCES

Between July 17 and August 2, 1945, the Big Three met again. These meetings took place just outside Berlin at Potsdam. There was a change of membership from Yalta. FDR had died, and was replaced by Harry Truman; Churchill had lost the July General Election, and was replaced by Clement Attlee.

What was decided at Potsdam?

German and Austrian borders

The precise borders of the four military occupation zones were agreed (see Source 2). The new border between Poland and Germany was called the Oder-Neisse line.

Treatment of Nazis

The Nazi Party was dissolved and a war crimes trial of former Nazis was to take place at Nuremberg, Germany.

Freedom in Germany

There would be free elections in Germany, along with a free press.

Reparations

Germany would pay war damages (reparations) to the Allies. Most would go to the USSR.

All Germans to live in Germany

German-speaking people living in Poland, Czechoslovakia, Hungary and Romania were to be expelled. They were forced to live in Germany.

HOW DID THE CONFERENCES AFFECT US-SOVIET RELATIONS?

Once it was clear Nazi Germany would be defeated, the old tensions between the USA and USSR re-emerged. These tensions were most clear over Poland and over free elections in Soviet-occupied Europe. Also, at Potsdam, President Truman told Stalin that the USA had successfully exploded an atom bomb. Immediately after Potsdam, Stalin ordered his nuclear scientists to build a Soviet atom bomb (see Source 1, p24). This increased tension. Truman added to this. He did not have the political skill of FDR in dealing with the USSR, and talked bluntly to the Soviet Foreign Minister, Molotov. This worsened relations between the USA and USSR.

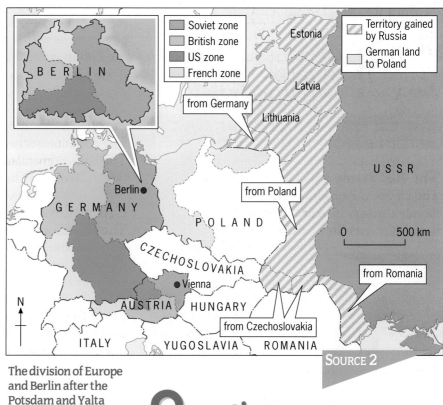

The division of Europe and Berlin after the Potsdam and Yalta Conferences.

SOURCE 2

Questions

1. Study Source 2. Where do you think there might be areas of conflict between the USSR and the Western powers? Explain your answer.
2. Which do you regard as the more successful conference: Yalta or Potsdam? Explain your answer.
3. In what ways did Yalta and Potsdam both help to increase tension between the USSR and the Western powers (Britain and the USA)?

Soviet expansion into Eastern Europe

In March 1946, Winston Churchill delivered a very important speech at the University of Missouri (see Source 1).

"A shadow has fallen upon the scenes so lately lighted by Allied victory. Nobody knows what Soviet Russia intends to do in the immediate future... From Stettin in the Baltic to Trieste in the Adriatic, an iron curtain has descended across the continent. Behind that line lie all the capitals of the ancient states of Central and Eastern Europe. This is certainly not the liberated Europe we fought to build up."

This famous 'Iron Curtain' speech vocalised what both the USA and Britain believed was taking place in Eastern Europe after 1945.

HOW DID THE USSR KEEP CONTROL OF EASTERN EUROPE AFTER 1945?

The Red Army
The USSR was able to control Eastern Europe mainly through its army. In 1944 and 1945 the Red Army overran all the countries in this area.

SOURCE 2   **The division between Eastern and Western Europe – Churchill's 'Iron Curtain'.**

Countries under communist control by 1948
Communist but independent
— Iron Curtain

At the Yalta Conference, Stalin had promised free elections for the countries it occupied. Elections took place in 1945 or 1946 in all the Eastern European countries. Communists won a great deal of votes (see Source 3). With the support of **socialists**, the communists were able to form governments in some countries, such as Hungary. These governments were supported by the Red Army, which was useful in keeping opposition quiet.

socialist
a person who believes in a more equal distribution of economic wealth

Poland's Lublin government
In Poland in 1945, communists formed a government with socialists. This was known as the Lublin government after the town in which it was formed. Once the communists obtained a majority share of government, they began forcing out non-communists. In 1947 they 'rigged' the election to gain complete power. The communists banned other political parties. They also controlled the press and media. The Soviet Red Army helped them keep power.

Czechoslovakia
The only Eastern European country with a democratic government after 1945 was Czechoslovakia. In the 1946 elections, the communists received only 47.6 per cent of the vote. With pressure from the USSR, the Prime Minister, Klement Gottwald, allowed communists to control the police and armed forces. In February 1948, the communists took over the government (see Source 3). In the process, a leading non-communist, Jan Masyrk, 'committed suicide' by falling from a window in the capital, Prague.

Cominform and Comecon
By 1949, all of Eastern Europe had communist governments. From 1947 these countries were linked with the USSR through Cominform (Communist Information Bureau). This meant that all communist governments in Eastern Europe had to take orders from the Soviet Communist Party. In 1949, Comecon (Council for Mutual Economic Assistance) was created.

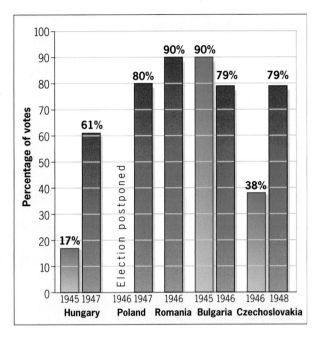

SOURCE 3 The percentage of votes for communists in Eastern Europe before and after 1946.

Under this, all communist governments had to create economic systems the same as the USSR. They were prohibited from trading with non-communist countries.

YUGOSLAVIA REJECTS SOVIET CONTROL

Only one communist government did not follow this path: Yugoslavia. It was ruled by Josip Tito. He had led the fight to free Yugoslavia from German occupation. He refused to accept control from the USSR. In 1948 Yugoslavia was thrown out of Cominform. From 1948 it was a communist country outside Soviet control.

WHY DID THE USSR WANT TO CONTROL EASTERN EUROPE?

World domination?
The USA and Britain believed that the USSR was planning to spread communism across Europe. The Soviet government had always stated that it wanted to make the whole world communist. To the West (Britain and the USA), control of Eastern Europe was the first step in this plan.

Defence
Stalin, however, was more interested in defending the USSR from future attack. Russia had been invaded on several occasions by foreign powers in recent history.

Moreover, in the Second World War, the USSR had suffered greatly. 20 million Soviets had died. Most of its industry and agriculture in western Russia had been destroyed. It was not in a position to attack other countries.

"We want friendly states around us"
Many of the countries of Eastern Europe had been allies of Germany. These included Hungary, Romania, Bulgaria, Slovakia and Croatia (part of Yugoslavia). The USSR wanted to have friendly governments on its western borders. The only way to do this was to make sure these governments were communist.

SOURCE 4 Two historians with different views on the origins of the Cold War.

(a) Adapted from *The Origins of the Cold War* by US historian Arthur Schlesinger, published in 1976.

'The Cold War was the brave response of free men to communist aggression. The West was faced at the end of the Second World War with the relentless drive for domination by the Soviet Union.'

(b) Adapted from *A Preponderance of Power* by US historian M. Leffler, published in 1992.

'Stalin preferred to concentrate on his own sphere of influence, Eastern Europe. His most provocative actions were reactions to Western policy in Germany. There is reason to give as much of the responsibility for the origins of the Cold War to the USA as to the USSR.'

Questions

1. Study Source 1. How reliable is this source as evidence of what happened to Europe after 1945?
2. Study Source 3. How did the USSR make sure Eastern Europe had communist governments after 1945? Explain your answer.
3. Study Source 4. These two historians give different reasons for Stalin's actions in Europe after 1945.
   a) In what ways are they different in their interpretation?
   b) Which interpretation do you regard as most truthful? Give reasons for your answer.

The Truman Doctrine and the Marshall Plan, 1947

BRITAIN'S FINANCIAL PROBLEMS

By 1947 Europe was divided into communist and non-communist-controlled blocs. An 'Iron Curtain' split Europe from north to south. However, in southeastern Europe, conflict between East and West was still taking place. In Greece there was civil war between communists and supporters of the Greek king. The king's side received help from Britain, who also supplied aid to Turkey.

Yet Britain found it increasingly difficult to support the fight against communism. Its economy was in a poor shape after the Second World War. It owed millions of dollars to the USA. Also, the winter of 1946-1947 was very severe. This caused an **energy crisis**.

energy crisis *shortage of coal, oil and gas for fuel and power*

This forced the British government to announce to the USA on February 21 that it couldn't afford to continue aiding Greece and Turkey.

THE TRUMAN DOCTRINE, 1947

President Truman decided to take over Britain's responsibilities. His speech to Congress (US parliament) became known as the Truman Doctrine. He stressed the threat of communism in Europe in order to obtain the money.

Truman did not mention the USSR or communists directly, but everyone knew what he was referring to. He planned to contain the development of communism. 'Containment' became the basis of US policy towards the USSR throughout the Cold War from 1947 to 1981.

SOURCE 1	President Truman's Speech to Congress on March 12, 1947, proposing the Truman Doctrine.

"At the present moment in history, nearly every nation must choose between alternative ways of life. The choice is often not a free one. One way of life is based upon the will of the majority, free elections, individual liberty, freedom of speech, and freedom from political tyranny. The second way of life is based upon the will of the minority forced upon the will of the majority. It relies upon terror, a controlled press and radio, and a lack of personal freedom. I believe it must be the policy of the USA to support peoples who resist being enslaved by armed minorities or outside pressures."

THE MARSHALL PLAN, 1947-1952

President Truman claimed that the Truman Doctrine and Marshall Plan were "two halves of the same walnut". The Plan was named after Truman's Secretary of State (Foreign Minister), George Marshall. Its official name was the European Recovery Plan (ERP). By 1947, Europe had still not recovered from the

WHAT WAS THE IMPACT OF THE TRUMAN DOCTRINE?

Aid to Greece and Turkey
Truman was able to get Congress to give immediate aid to Greece and Turkey.

Creation of the CIA
Congress passed the National Security Act. This created the Central Intelligence Agency (CIA). This agency would become the main US force to help contain communism.

Creation of the NSA
The Act also created the National Security Agency (NSA). This agency controlled spying equipment like spy planes, ships, and satellites.

Creation of the NSC
The Act also created the National Security Council (NSC). This was a committee of top military and defence advisers to the President. It became the most important committee advising the President on military affairs.

Compulsory military service in the USA
In 1948 the Selective Service Act became law. This made military service compulsory in peacetime for the first time in US history.

McCarthyism
Fear of communism grew within the USA. A Republican Senator, Joseph McCarthy, exploited this. From the late 1940s to 1954 he claimed that there were communists in every type of job within America, in Hollywood, and even in government. Many Americans lost their jobs because others feared they might be communists.

WHAT WAS THE IMPACT OF THE MARSHALL PLAN ON EUROPE?

Aided European recovery

The economic aid provided by the Marshall Plan made a huge difference to European recovery. The USA provided all types of aid: food; livestock for farms; tractors; lorries and factory equipment. By 1952, unemployment had dropped dramatically all over Western Europe. Agricultural production rose, and by the early 1950s, rationing had come to an end in Britain.

Stopped spread of communism

Politically, the Marshall Plan helped stop the spread of communism. Although communist parties were large in France and Italy, they never led either government throughout the Cold War period.

Forced Soviet creation of Cominform and Comecon

The Marshall Plan was rejected by the USSR (see Source 3). It forced the Soviets to set up its own organisations. In 1947 Cominform (Communist Information Bureau) was created. It forced all communist parties in Europe to follow Moscow's orders. In 1949 Comecon was created. This was a trading organisation of all communist countries. They could trade with each other, but not non-communist countries.

devastation of the Second World War. Economic hardship led to growth in support for communism. Both France and Italy had very large communist parties. The USA feared that, if economic recovery did not come quickly, communism would spread rapidly in Western Europe. Therefore, Marshall suggested enormous economic aid to Europe to contain communism.

The Marshall Plan was not directed against the USSR. The USA was willing to offer the USSR and its communist allies Marshall Aid. However, the USSR made sure that no communist country would receive American aid. The USSR was suspicious of America's motives. So, between 1947 and 1952, Marshall Aid only went to Western, non-communist Europe. In total, $13.2 billion was given. This made Marshall Aid the biggest peacetime aid programme in world history.

So, by the end of 1947, the split between communist and non-communist Europe was worse than ever.

SOURCE 2 A German poster on the Marshall Plan, 1948. The lorry has 'ERP' (European Recovery Plan) on its bonnet. *Freie Bahn* is German for 'free road'. The lorry is passing the German border: *zoll* means 'customs'.

SOURCE 3 In September 1947, Soviet Deputy Foreign Minister, Andrei Vyshinsky, gave the United Nations General Assembly his opinion on the Marshall Plan.

"This Plan is an attempt to split Europe into two camps. It is part of a plan to create a bloc of countries in Europe hostile to the USSR."

Questions

1. Study Source 1. How useful is it to an historian writing about the Cold War? Explain your answer.
2. Study Source 2. How useful is this poster in explaining European views towards the Marshall Plan? Give reasons for your answer.
3. Study Source 3. How reliable is it as evidence of why the Marshall Plan was introduced? Give reasons for your answer.
4. Why were the Truman Doctrine and the Marshall Plan "two halves of the same walnut"? Explain your answer.

The Berlin Airlift crisis, 1948-49

The first big test for the USA's policy of containment came over Berlin. In 1945 Germany had been divided into four military occupation zones. These were controlled by the USA, the USSR, Britain and France. Each zone had its own military force. Berlin, the capital of Germany under Hitler, was also divided into four military zones. However, Berlin was a long way inside the Soviet military zone of occupation (see Source 2, p11). To get to their military zones, the British, Americans and French had to use specially assigned roads, rail links or canals.

WHAT CAUSED THE BERLIN AIRLIFT CRISIS?

The Deutschmark and Trizonia

By 1946 tension between the USSR and the Western powers (USA, Britain and France) was growing. Britain and the USA wanted Germany to become economically strong. The USSR wanted Germany to stay weak and divided. To make their areas economically stronger, the USA and Britain decided to introduce a new currency. The old currency was very weak. The new currency was to be the Deutschmark. This became the currency in the British and American zones of Germany in December 1946. This created the area known as Bizonia (two zones). In February 1948, the French zone joined to form Trizonia.

The Deutschmark in Berlin

This alarmed the USSR, which saw a reunited, strong Germany as a threat. What created the greatest alarm was the Western decision to extend the Deutschmark to their zones in Berlin on June 23, 1948. From that date Berlin had two currencies – one in the Soviet sector, and one in the three Western sectors. Soon Berliners found that the Deutschmark was worth more than the Soviet zone mark.

Stalin's reaction

Stalin, the Soviet leader, reacted aggressively. He closed off all land routes into Western Berlin. Three and a half million Berliners were now trapped 110 miles from Western-controlled Germany. Stalin hoped this tactic would force the Western allies out of Berlin.

WHAT WAS THE AIRLIFT?

With all road, rail and canal links cut, the only way of reaching Western-controlled Berlin was by air. In 1945 the USSR had agreed that the Western allies could use three air corridors, each 20 miles wide, to reach Western Berlin. The Western allies could use two Berlin airports: Templehof and Gatow. They could also land seaplanes on Lake Havel, in Berlin.

President Truman and British Prime Minister Attlee decided to overcome the land blockade, and keep their part of Berlin supplied by air. This would involve sending 2,000 tonnes of supplies every day. The biggest planes the allies had could carry ten tonnes of supplies. This meant that the plan to supply Berlin would be a round-the-clock activity. The USA called their plan to beat the blockade Operation Vittle ('vittles' is another version of the English word 'victuals', meaning food).

HOW SUCCESSFUL WAS THE AIRLIFT?

Every day planes flew into Berlin. When winter came, the allies had to airlift in coal and fuel supplies. On Easter Sunday, a record 24,000 tonnes of supplies was airlifted in within 24 hours.

The Soviet armed forces did not shoot down any planes. If they had, it would have been regarded as an act of war. Instead, they flew their fighters close to Western cargo planes in order to intimidate them. During the airlift, 79 British and American pilots lost their lives in accidents. 278,000 flights were made, carrying 2.3 million tonnes of supplies. Coal made up two thirds of the supplies. The cost of the airlift to the Western allies was $200 million.

On May 12, 1949, the USSR called off the blockade. They had failed to stop the Western allies supplying their part of Berlin. It was the first great victory for containment. President Truman had stood up to Stalin and the USSR. However, the Berlin Airlift crisis made sure that Germany would be divided. In 1949 the three

SOURCE 1 A cartoon from the British magazine, *Punch*. It shows the Soviet leader, Stalin, with a gun. The US and British planes are shown as storks, birds usually associated with bringing newborn babies to their families.

SOURCE 2 *"It was amazing, all the things they brought over in their planes. I still remember my youngest boy was there when the Americans dropped little parachutes from the planes with sweets, chewing gum and chocolate."*

Hildegarde Herrberger, a Berliner, remembers the airlift.

SOURCE 3

Members of the US Air Force hand out gifts and food in Operation Santa Claus, Christmas 1948.

. . . . FACT FILE . . . .

SUPPLIES DELIVERED TO BERLIN DURING THE AIRLIFT (TONNES)

Commodity	USA	Britain
Coal	1.4 million	164,000
Food	296,000	241,000
Military supplies	–	18,000
Others	65,000	25,000
Petrol	–	92,000
TOTAL	1.7 million	542,000
TOTAL COMBINED	**2.3 million tonnes**	

INVESTIGATE...
How would you have responded to the Berlin Airlift if you had been Josef Stalin? Play his role at
http://edition.cnn.com/SPECIALS/cold.war/episodes/04
Go to the section entitled 'Brinkmanship'.

Questions

1. Study Source 1. What statement is this cartoon trying to make about the Berlin Airlift?
2. Study Sources 2 and 3. Do they fully explain what the Berlin Airlift was like? Give reasons for your answer.
3. Look at the Fact File on the tonnage of supplies flown to West Berlin during the airlift. What can you learn about the airlift from it?
4. 'The Berlin Airlift crisis was caused by Britain and the USA rather than the USSR.' Do you agree with this statement? Explain your answer, using information and sources in this section.

Western zones were united to form the Federal Republic of Germany, known as West Germany. The Soviet zones formed another country called the German Democratic Republic, known as East Germany. Berlin was still stranded deep in East Germany. The country remained divided until November 1989.

A continent divided: NATO and the Warsaw Pact

WHAT IS NATO?

One of the most important consequences of the Berlin Airlift Crisis was the formation of NATO (North Atlantic Treaty Organisation). It was formed and signed on April 1949. From September 1949 each member agreed that, if any one member were attacked, all the others would join to defend it. 12 countries signed the original treaty.

> **SOURCE 1**
>
> The North Atlantic Treaty, 1949. This created NATO.
>
> 'Article 1 of the Treaty.
>
> The Parties undertake… to settle any international disputes by peaceful means.'
>
> 'Article 5 of the Treaty.
>
> The Parties agree that an armed attack on one or more of them shall be considered an attack against them all.'

NATO was the first peacetime military alliance in US history. Its creation showed that the USA was willing to stand up to Soviet aggression. Permanent American military bases were established in Western Europe. The main US bases were in Britain. During the Berlin Airlift Crisis (see p16) the USA moved B29 bombers to Britain. These planes could deliver nuclear weapons. This became very important from April 1949, when the USSR successfully exploded its first atom bomb. From then on, there was always the risk of nuclear war between East and West.

WHAT WAS NSC 68?

NSC 68 (US National Security Council document no. 68) was produced in 1950. It called for a massive increase in US military spending. The reason was increasing American fear of the threat of communism. In 1949, not only had the USSR obtained an atom bomb, but China had also become communist (see p56). So, by 1949, not only was the world's largest country (the USSR) communist – so was the world's most populous (700 million), China.

American fear of communism increased when the Korean War broke out in 1950 (see p22). McCarthyism heightened US paranoia. As a result, US military spending rose from $1 billion a year in 1949 to $50 billion in 1953. US military forces were stationed all around the world in a bid to stop communist aggression.

WEST GERMAN REARMAMENT, 1955

To increase the military forces of NATO, the US and British decided to let West Germany rearm. This would mean less money would be spent by Britain and the USA on the defence of Western Europe. In 1955 West Germany was allowed to join NATO and have a large army and air force. However, it could not control any nuclear weapons. British, French and US troops continued to be based in West Germany to stop Soviet aggression.

SOURCE 2

A Soviet cartoon of NATO, from 1952.

WHAT WAS THE WARSAW PACT?

The USSR saw West Germany's admission to NATO as a threat, believing it would give rise to a new Nazi Germany. It retaliated by creating the Warsaw Pact. This was created in Warsaw, Poland, on May 1, 1955, one week after West Germany joined NATO. It was an Eastern European version of NATO, made up of all Eastern Europe's communist states, except Yugoslavia.

The Warsaw Pact was dominated by the USSR. All Warsaw Pact armed forces followed Soviet orders. All used Soviet weapons.

EUROPE DIVIDED THROUGH GERMANY

From 1955 Europe was divided into two armed camps – NATO and the Warsaw Pact. Each had nuclear weapons. The frontline between these two military alliances was central Germany. The border between East and West Germany became the most heavily defended in the world.

CENTO AND SEATO

However, the military rivalry between the USA and USSR soon covered much of the world. The USA helped increase tension by setting up versions of NATO in Asia. CENTO (Central Treaty Organisation) was based in the Middle East. SEATO (South East Asian Treaty Organisation) was based in South East Asia. The USA aimed to surround the USSR and communist China with military alliances. The military confrontation between the two sides involved a wide variety of weapons. Large ground forces were based in Europe, backed up by air forces. By the late 1950s both sides owned nuclear missiles. These could reach both the USA and USSR. The Cold War had developed into a global conflict, in which the whole world faced nuclear destruction if a war broke out.

... FACT FILE ...

MEMBERS OF THE WARSAW PACT

USSR Poland Hungary
Romania Bulgaria
Czechoslovakia Albania
East Germany
Albania left in 1968

SOURCE 4

International military alliances in 1955.

SOURCE 3

From the Warsaw Pact, May 1, 1955.

'The integration of West Germany into NATO increases the threat of war. Therefore the peace-loving states of Europe should take the necessary measures for safeguarding their security and maintaining European peace.

Article 1 of the Pact.

The Parties undertake… not to threaten or use force to settle international disputes.'

'Article 4 of the Pact.

In the event of an armed attack in Europe on one or more of the countries of the Pact, the other countries in the Pact will resist attack, including armed force.'

Questions

1. Study Sources 1 and 3. In what ways are they similar? Give reasons for your answer.
2. Study Source 2.
   a) What statement is it trying to make about NATO?
   b) As it is a Soviet cartoon, is it completely unreliable? Explain your answer.
3. Study Source 4. How far was the USSR surrounded by US-led military alliances?
4. How far was US fear of communism the main reason for the growth of both NATO and the Warsaw Pact? Explain your answer using information and sources from this section.

The origins of the Cold War

In a GCSE History examination candidates are asked several types of questions. These include:

- The evaluation of sources
- The evaluation of sources using your own knowledge
- Writing extended answers using your own knowledge

A fourth type is the structured question. In this type of question candidates are asked to use only their own knowledge to write an answer. The answers are similar to extended writing answers but tend to be shorter.

QUESTIONS AND DARRYL'S ANSWERS

(a) What was agreed at the Potsdam Conference, 1945?

(4 marks)

In 1945 the wartime Allies met at Potsdam. There were two meetings. At the first, Churchill represented Britain, Truman represented the USA, and Stalin represented the USSR. At the second meeting, Attlee represented Britain instead of Churchill. The Allies agreed to divide up Germany into four zones of occupation: one each for the USA, the USSR, Britain, and France. Poland was given lands in eastern Germany because it lost some of its eastern territory to the USSR.

(b) Explain why the USA introduced the Marshall Plan.

(6 marks)

The USA introduced the Marshall Plan in 1947. It was meant to be part of the US plan to contain communism in Europe. The other part of the plan was the Truman Doctrine. The Plan was called the European Recovery Plan. It was named after the US Secretary of State, George Marshall.

Europe was in a mess in 1947. It was still suffering hardship after the war. There were food shortages and unemployment. Because of this, communist parties became popular in Western Europe. France and Italy had very large communist parties.

The Marshall Plan gave economic aid to countries in Europe who wanted it. It was even offered to communist countries in Eastern Europe, but Stalin refused to accept aid. For five years after 1947, billions of US dollars were sent to Europe. It brought about economic recovery and prevented the spread of communism.

(c) 'The most important cause of the Cold War was the suspicion and rivalry between Truman and Stalin.'
Do you agree with this statement? Explain your answer.

(10 marks)

After the Second World War, the USA and the USSR became enemies. The Cold War had started. An important reason for this was that the USA and the USSR had different political and economic systems. The USA was a capitalist country. This meant that business and property was privately owned. The USA was also a democracy. People had freedom of speech. The USSR was a communist state. All business and property was owned by the government. It was a dictatorship. There was no freedom of speech. Each country distrusted the other. This had been the case since the communist Revolution of 1917. It was only the common fear of Hitler that forced them to be allies between 1941 and 1945. Another reason was the distrust caused by the Yalta Conference of 1945. Stalin had promised free elections in Eastern Europe. Instead, he created communist dictatorships.

Truman disliked communism. He wanted to stop its spread. In 1947 he produced the Truman Doctrine. He aimed to contain communism in Eastern Europe. To defend Europe against communism, he helped create Bizonia in the British and American zones of Germany in 1948. This forced Stalin to blockade western Berlin in 1948. The Berlin Airlift of 1948-49 made the Cold War more dangerous. It was caused by suspicion between Truman and Stalin. After it, Truman helped found NATO. This was an organisation to stop the spread of communism. It also helped make the Cold War more dangerous. So, the suspicion and rivalry between Truman and Stalin was an important cause of the Cold War.

Question (a)

This question requires candidates to show their knowledge of a historical event.

Darryl mentions several points, including the names of those who represented the Allies at the Conference. While this might be interesting, it doesn't directly answer the question. However, Darryl does mention some important points agreed at Potsdam, such as the Polish-German frontier and the division of Germany into zones of military occupation. He doesn't mention the issue of reparations after the war, or the fact that Potsdam confirmed many of the decisions made at Yalta. Moreover, although he refers to the new Polish-German border, he doesn't provide sufficient detailed information, such as reference to the Oder-Neisse line.

As a result, Darryl was awarded 2 out of a possible 4 marks.

Question (b)

This question also aims to test candidates' own knowledge of events in the Cold War.

Darryl's answer is much better here. He is able to identify the reasons why the Marshall Plan was introduced. He links this directly to the US policy of containment of communism within Europe. He also links the Marshall Plan to the Truman Doctrine. Truman called these "two halves of the same walnut". Darryl links this effectively to the problems facing Europe after the war, in particular acute economic problems like food shortages and unemployment. These were problems that the USA was able to exploit to gain support for their cause. Again, Darryl is able to link economic aid to preventing the spread of communism. Finally, Darryl goes somewhat beyond the demands of the question by mentioning the impact of the Marshall Pan.

As a result, Darryl was awarded 5 out of a possible 6 marks.

Question (c)

This question requires candidates to identify a variety of reasons for the Cold War. In addition, they will need to comment on the importance of the relationship between Truman and Stalin in causing the Cold War.

Darryl identifies a number of reasons for the Cold War. The long-term hostility, dating back to 1917, is mentioned at the start. Unfortunately, the structure of the answer suggests initially that Darryl is writing a general essay about the causes of the Cold War. It would have been far better had Darryl dealt with the rivalry of Truman and Stalin first, then identified and explained other reasons for the outbreak of the Cold War. This structure would have been more in line with the 'agree or disagree' aspect of the question.

However, later in his answer, Darryl does mention how Truman and Stalin's rivalry did make the Cold War worse. In particular, he identifies the events surrounding the Berlin Airlift crisis of 1948-9. But, whilst Darryl does state that their rivalry was an important cause of the Cold War, he does not assess whether their rivalry was the most important cause or not.

If Darryl had structured his answer into a 'agree or disagree' format, and had mentioned what he regarded as the most important cause, and why, he would have achieved full marks. As a result, Darryl was awarded 7 out of a possible 10 marks.

EXTENSION WORK

Who do you think was more to blame for the start of the Cold War: the USA or the USSR? Explain your answer, **using information and sources from the last chapter**.

(15 marks)

• OCR accepts no responsibility whatsoever for the accuracy or method of working in the anwers given.

The Cold War gets hot: Korea, 1950-53

The Cold War began in Europe. However, the first major armed conflict took place in the Far East, in Korea.

WHY WAS KOREA DIVIDED?

Korea had been part of the Japanese Empire from 1910 to 1945. When Japan was defeated, Korea was occupied by troops from the USSR and the USA. The USSR occupied land north of the 38°N latitude line (see Source 4). The USA occupied the area south of that line. In the South, the USA created a non-communist government, called the Republic of Korea. It was created on August 15, 1948. In the North, the USSR created a communist government, called the Democratic Republic of Korea. It was created on September 9, 1948. Eventually, it was hoped that the two parts of Korea would be reunited.

WHY WAS KOREA IMPORTANT IN THE COLD WAR?

Korea became very important to the USA due to events in China. From 1927 to 1949 there was a civil war in China. Communist troops fought Nationalist troops in a struggle to take control of the country. The only break in this conflict took place between 1937 and 1945, when both sides fought the invading Japanese. By 1949, the Communists had won, driving the Nationalists onto the island of Taiwan. The USA now feared the spread of communism across East Asia. As in Europe, containment would be essential because eventually Japan (a US ally) might be threatened by communism.

WHY DID THE KOREAN WAR BEGIN?

The United Nations tried to keep peace in Korea. There was the promise of nationwide elections as the start of a process to reunite the country. Was Korea going to be communist or non-communist? On June 25, 1950, in a bid to unite Korea without elections, the communist North attacked the South. Using Soviet military equipment, Northern troops quickly overran the South and captured the capital, Seoul. By September the war seemed to be almost over.

> **SOURCE 1** From an interview with Yan Von Sik, a member of the 1950 North Korean Army.
>
> *"We believed that we had to fight for our motherland, for our people, for our leader Kim Il Sung. We believed it would be better to liberate the South and to unify Korea. That's what we were fighting for."*

What turned the Korean War into a major war was the intervention of the United Nations. The USA took advantage of a Soviet boycott of the UN in mid-summer 1950 to gain UN support for military intervention. Led by the USA, the United Nations sent troops to help South Korea. By the end of the war, countries like Greece, Turkey and Ethiopia had sent support to South Korea. However, the major force was provided by the USA and Britain.

> **SOURCE 2** Historian John Patrick Diggins's view of why the USA became involved in the Korean War. Adapted from *The Proud Decades*, published in 1989.
>
> 'President Truman immediately interpreted the invasion by the North as an act of aggression that must be resisted. Unless resisted, other communist leaders might take similar actions. This would lead to World War III.'

> **SOURCE 3** From a speech given by British Prime Minister, Clement Attlee, in 1953, on why Britain supported the UN forces in Korea.
>
> *"If the United Nations organisation was not to [fail to prevent aggression among members, as in] the old League of Nations, it was necessary that a halt to aggression be called."*

HOW DID GENERAL MACARTHUR CHANGE THE KOREAN WAR?

Initial victory
The UN had entered the war to stop the North taking over the South. It appointed American General Douglas MacArthur as Commander-in-Chief of UN forces. MacArthur had been a prominent American general in the defeat of Japan. He came up with a daring plan to defeat

THE KOREAN STALEMATE

Although Seoul was recaptured by UN troops on March 14, 1951, they could not push the Chinese and North Koreans back from the 38°N latitude line. Fighting continued for another two years with neither side making a breakthrough. On June 23, 1951, ceasefire (armistice) talks began at Kaesong. The talks then moved to Panmunjom on the front line between North and South. It was only in 1953 that a ceasefire was finally agreed.

Officially the war in Korea has never ended. Armistice talks have taken place every week since 1953. The border between North and South Korea remains one of the most heavily defended on earth. During the Korean War, 50,000 US troops were killed. The numbers of Koreans killed has not been calculated accurately, but is estimated to be at least three million.

Like the Berlin Airlift (see p16), the Korean War showed that the USA would not stand for the extension of communism across the globe. Like the Iron Curtain in Europe, a 'Bamboo Curtain' had descended across Asia. On one side was communist China and North Korea. What the USA feared was the growth of communism elsewhere in Asia.

North Korea. He decided to land UN troops far behind enemy lines. On September 15, 1950, he landed troops at Inchon, near Seoul. This caught the North Koreans completely by surprise. The landing threatened to cut off their troops in the South. They retreated. UN forces recaptured all of South Korea.

A step too far?

Instead of ending the war, MacArthur decided to invade the North. He captured the northern capital, Pyongyang, and sent his troops to capture all North Korea. Even though he was warned to keep away from the Chinese border, MacArthur's troops approached it at the Yalu River. On November 25, 1950, the character of the war was altered dramatically. 500,000 Chinese communist volunteers poured into North Korea. They drove UN forces back into the South and, once again, captured Seoul.

MacArthur wanted to use nuclear weapons against the Chinese and to extend the war to communist China. To prevent a major world war, President Truman dismissed MacArthur. He was replaced by General Matthew Ridgeway on April 12.

Questions

1. Produce a timeline of the main events surrounding the Korean War, from 1945 to 1953.
2. Study Sources 1, 2 and 3.
   a) Why do they each provide a different view on why the Korean War developed? Give reasons for your answer.
   b) Which source do you think gives the most accurate view about why the war developed? Give reasons for your answer.
3. 'US General MacArthur was the main reason that the Korean War lasted such a long time.' Do you agree with this statement? Explain your answer, using information and sources from this section.

USA v USSR: the arms race and the space race

SUPERPOWER RIVALRY

The rivalry between the USA and the USSR took many forms during the Cold War. Both sides had nuclear, biological and chemical weapons. Equally, both sides had plans to explore space. Most importantly of all, both sides wanted to show the world that their way of life was the better one. Neither wished to appear inferior. Each feared the other, and both wanted to possess the best possible protection against attack. They strived to develop newer and better weapons and space technology for these reasons. This became known as the 'arms race' and the 'space race'.

RIVALRY AS PROPAGANDA

This rivalry played a major role in each nation's propaganda. Both the USA and the USSR wanted to influence countries in the Third World, to win them over to their way of life. The country with the most powerful armed forces had a better chance of impressing and influencing Third World countries. The same was true of the space race. Both the USA and the USSR sent satellites and men into space from 1957. Success was seen as an important sign of a superior economy and society. This was attractive to poverty-stricken Third World nations.

THE NUCLEAR ARMS RACE

What was the importance of the nuclear arms race?

The arms race between the USA and USSR lasted the whole length of the Cold War. In 1945 the USSR had the largest army in the world. The USA had the largest navy and air force. From 1945 to 1949, the USA had another advantage. It had nuclear weapons and was the only country ever to have used them. US atom bombs (A-bombs) were dropped on Japan in August 1945. In 1949 the USSR exploded its first A-bomb. From 1949 both countries raced to develop the most devastating nuclear weapons.

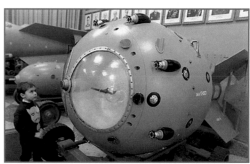

SOURCE 1 A child inspects an early Soviet A-bomb in a Russian museum in the 1990s.

In the early 1950s, the USA tested a weapon more powerful than the atom bomb – the hydrogen bomb (H-bomb). The USSR then acquired a H-bomb. To add to the equation, Britain also acquired nuclear weapons in the 1950s. By the end of the Cold War in 1991, France, India, China, Pakistan and Israel also had nuclear weapons.

> **· · · · · · · · FACT FILE · · · · · · · · ·**
>
> **HOW DOES AN A-BOMB DIFFER FROM A H-BOMB?**
> An atom bomb is based on nuclear fission.
> A uranium atom is split. This releases enormous energy, which causes a nuclear explosion.
> A hydrogen bomb is based on nuclear fusion. Two hydrogen atoms are forced together. This causes an even greater nuclear explosion. If a H-bomb landed on London, its effects would be felt 600 miles away – for example in Madrid, Spain.

SOURCE 2 The USA explodes its first H-bomb on Eniwetok Island, in the Pacific.

How did nuclear weapons develop?

During the 1950s the delivery system of nuclear weapons changed. In 1945 they were dropped from a plane. By the end of the 1950s they could be delivered as guided missiles. The most powerful missiles were called ICBMs (Inter-Continental Ballistic Missiles). They could send nuclear warheads between the USA and the USSR. In the 1960s, the USA was the first to develop submarine-launched nuclear missiles. Finally, in the 1980s, US President Reagan attempted to place satellites in space that could shoot down nuclear missiles. This was called SDI (Strategic Defence Initiative; see p67). It was never installed.

How did US and Soviet policy on nuclear weapons change?

From 1953 to 1961, the USA pursued a policy of 'brinkmanship'. It threatened to use nuclear weapons if either the USSR or communist China threatened to spread communism. This meant that the world was constantly on the brink of nuclear war. However, from 1961 to 1991, both US and Soviet policy became focused around the concept of M.A.D. (Mutually Assured Destruction). Both sides had so many nuclear weapons that the use of them by one would result in the complete destruction of both.

THE SPACE RACE

Both the USA and the USSR wanted to prove that they were the most technologically advanced country. An important part of this rivalry became space exploration.

The USSR

The USSR was the most successful in the early stages of the space race. In 1957 the Soviets shocked the USA and the world by successfully launching a space satellite. This was called *Sputnik*. Shortly afterwards, the Soviets were able to send dogs into space in specially designed rockets. Finally, in 1961, the USSR was the first country to send a man into space: Yuri Gagarin. Soviet leader, Nikita Khrushchev, claimed that Soviet successes in space proved the superiority of the communist system.

The USA

In 1961, US President John F. Kennedy had said to the American people, "I believe that this nation should commit itself to achieving the goal, before the decade is out, of landing a man on the Moon." Although the USA was less successful than the USSR in the late 1950s and early 1960s, it did achieve Kennedy's goal. In 1969, Neil Armstrong became the first human to set foot on the Moon. However, rivalry continued.

SOURCE 3	The balance of nuclear weapons produced by the USA and USSR in the 1960s.

Bar chart comparing USA and USSR nuclear weapons, 1960–1969.
USA/USSR values: 1960: 18/35; 1961: 63/50; 1962: 294/75; 1963: 424/100; 1964: 834/200; 1965: 854/270; 1966: 904/300; 1967: 1054/460; 1968: 1054/800; 1969: 1054/1050.

SOURCE 4	Tom Denchy, a member of a US ICBM crew.

'We felt that the Soviets were trying to take over the world. We were one of the largest stumbling blocks stopping them.'

General Mikhail Mokrinski, Soviet nuclear bomber pilot.

'The Americans were the aggressors who wanted to conquer the whole world. We had to protect the world.'

Questions

1. Study Source 4. Does it fully explain why the arms race developed between the USA and the USSR during the Cold War? Explain your answer.
2. Why do you think the space race was important to both the USA and the USSR during the Cold War?
3. 'The arms race between the USA and USSR was the most dangerous aspect of the Cold War.' Do you agree with this statement? Explain your answer, using information and sources from this section.

The Hungarian Uprising, 1956

In 1946, Winston Churchill had said that Europe was divided by an 'iron curtain'. Behind that curtain, communist governments had been established in the areas of Europe liberated by the Soviet army in 1944-1945. In these states, the communist government controlled almost every aspect of life. All businesses were owned by the government. Every citizen was an employee of the state. There was no democracy and no freedom of speech. The government also persecuted those who openly tried to practise religion because **atheism** was essential to communism.

atheism
the belief that there is no God

In 1953 the first open opposition to communist rule broke out in East Germany – in East Berlin. This was easily crushed by the police and the army. However, by 1956, a major change seemed to be taking place in the USSR, which influenced how the other countries in the Soviet bloc were run.

CHANGES IN THE SOVIET LEADERSHIP

In March 1953 Stalin, the ruler of the USSR, died. He was an absolute dictator and had ruled with an iron fist since 1924. When he died, the head of the KGB, Lavrenti Beria, tried to take power. He was arrested and executed by other members of the Soviet government. Stalin's place was briefly taken by another member of the government, Malenkov. However, it soon became clear that the government was actually being run by two other Soviet officials, Nikolai Bulganin and Nikita Khrushchev. Khrushchev was General Secretary of the Communist Party. He eventually became sole ruler (Premier) of the USSR in 1958.

AUSTRIAN STATE TREATY, 1955

In 1955, the USSR agreed to sign the Austrian State Treaty. This was an agreement with the USA, Britain and France. All four countries agreed to remove their armed forces from Austria. From 1955 Austria would be a neutral country. This was the first time the USSR voluntarily agreed to remove troops from a country. This act gave hope to people behind the Iron Curtain in Eastern Europe: they might be able to break free from Soviet influence.

20TH CONGRESS OF THE SOVIET COMMUNIST PARTY, 1956

In February 1956, Khrushchev made a remarkable speech at the Communist Party Congress. In a secret meeting he criticised Stalin. He claimed that Stalin had taken too much power. He suggested that greater freedom should be allowed within the USSR. This news soon became public knowledge in the USSR and in other communist countries.

UPRISING IN POLAND, 1956

News of Khrushchev's speech was greeted with hope in other communist countries. Many believed that they would be allowed more freedom. These groups were soon disappointed. In Poznan, Poland, in June 1956, rioting took place against communist rule. Over 100 people were killed. The riots led to the appointment of a new Prime Minister, Wladislaw Gomulka, but not to a change in communist rule.

THE HUNGARIAN UPRISING, OCTOBER 1956

The most serious disturbance took place in Hungary in October 1956. Up until Stalin's death, Hungary was ruled by Mátyás Rákosi. He was a tyrant very similar to Stalin and had been responsible for the death and imprisonment of over 100,000 Hungarians. When Stalin died, Rákosi was replaced as Prime Minister of Hungary by Imré Nagy. Nagy was seen as a moderate and was Prime Minister from 1953 to 1955.

In October 1956, serious rioting against communist rule broke out in the capital, Budapest. On October 24, Nagy was appointed Prime Minister again. Fighting took place between ordinary Hungarians and Soviet armed forces based in Hungary.

Faced with the almost complete collapse of communist rule, the USSR had to take action. The Soviet Army entered Hungary by force.

Street fighting occurred in Budapest. Between November 4 and 11, 7,000 Soviet troops were killed. Thirty thousand Hungarians died. Thousands fled over the border into neutral Austria. Nagy was imprisoned and later executed in 1958. He was replaced by a loyal communist, János Kádár.

During the fighting the Hungarian rebels appealed for help from the USA. None came. The USA was unwilling to upset the split in Central Europe between communist and non-communist countries. The USSR had repaired the tear in the Iron Curtain.

A Hungarian freedom fighter in Budapest, 1956.

SOURCE 1

A Hungarian tank passes a burnt-out Soviet tank in Budapest during the 1956 uprising.

SOURCE 5

From Seftan Delmer of the *Daily Express* newspaper in Budapest, October 23, 1956.

'I have been the witness today of one of the great events of history. I have seen people in Budapest come out into the streets in open rebellion against their Soviet overlords. I have marched with them and almost wept for joy. And the great point about the rebellion is that it looks like being successful.'

SOURCE 2

From an interview with Major Grigori Dobrynov, part of the Soviet Army in 1956.

"We were told to get ready to re-enter Budapest because the terror had started. We were not a force of occupation. Instead, we were going in as saviours to protect the people from terrorism."

SOURCE 3

A radio broadcast by Imré Nagy, Hungarian Prime Minister, November 4, 1956.

"This is the Hungarian Prime Minister Imré Nagy speaking. At dawn Soviet troops attacked our country in order to overthrow the Hungarian democratic government."

Questions

1. Study Sources 2 and 3.
   a) Why do they offer different accounts of the Hungarian Uprising? Explain your answer.
   b) Which one do you regard as the more truthful? Give reasons for your answer.
2. Study Source 5. How reliable is this account of the Hungarian Uprising? Explain your answer.
3. 'The Hungarian Uprising was doomed from the start.' Do you agree with this statement? Explain your answer, using information and sources in this section.

The big freeze: the Berlin Wall crisis, 1961

Berlin was a centre of tension throughout the Cold War. The city had been divided into four military sectors at the end of the Second World War. The USSR, USA, Britain and France all had troops in Berlin. Yet Berlin itself was in the heart of Soviet-controlled East Germany. Already, in 1948-1949, Berlin had been the centre of extreme tension with the failed Soviet attempt to blockade West Berlin.

In 1958 talks began between the USSR and the Western powers about the future of Berlin. The USSR wanted the three Western powers to leave West Berlin. The Western powers instead wanted to have talks about uniting East and West Germany. No progress was made.

WHY DID A CRISIS DEVELOP OVER BERLIN BETWEEN 1960 AND 1961?

East Germans crossing to West Berlin

The border between East and West Germany was heavily guarded by troops and police. Barbed wire, minefields and watchtowers made sure no one could travel from East to West. The only exception was Berlin. There were no border controls between the four military sectors within the city. As a result, thousands of East Germans could flee to West Germany merely by crossing from East to West Berlin. From 1949 to 1961, 2.6 million out of a population of 17 million had fled East Germany to the West. East Germany was the only country in Europe with a declining population!

The U2 incident, May 1960

In May 1960 a major international incident occurred. A US U2 spy plane was shot down over the USSR. Pilots of U2 planes were meant to avoid capture by committing suicide. However, the pilot, Gary Powers, was captured. At a press conference US President Eisenhower denied the USA sent spy planes over Soviet territory. Soviet Premier Khrushchev then announced to the world that they had captured Gary Powers. This proved

Eisenhower was lying. Tension increased when Eisenhower refused to apologise.

Cuba, 1961

In spring 1961, a crisis developed between the USA and Cuba (see p32). US-backed Cuban rebels tried to overthrow the pro-communist government of Fidel Castro. They failed badly at the Bay of Pigs. This was seen as a great humiliation for the USA and, in particular, for its new President, John F. Kennedy. It also made the Soviet Premier, Khrushchev, think he could bully the USA into leaving West Berlin.

THE BERLIN WALL IS BUILT

In June 1961 Khrushchev met Kennedy in Vienna, Austria. At the meeting, Khrushchev felt Kennedy was young and inexperienced. The Soviet leader thought he could use this to his advantage. So, on August 13, 1961, the East German government, backed by the USSR, closed the border in Berlin. East German guards put up a barbed wire fence all around West Berlin. On August 15 they began constructing a wall that separated West Berlin from East Berlin

SOURCE 1   Berlin and the Berlin Wall in 1961.

EAST GERMANY — Berlin Wall — EAST GERMANY — French zone — Checkpoint Charlie — British zone — EAST BERLIN — WEST BERLIN — Soviet zone — US zone — N — EAST GERMANY — 0   10 km and East Germany (see Source 1). West Berlin was now an island of Western capitalism, with its own currency, in the middle of the communist bloc of Eastern Europe. The last gap in the Iron Curtain was closed.

The East Germans called it the Anti-Fascist Defence Wall. 'Fascist' was a term linked to Hitler and the Nazis. The USSR suggested that the Wall would keep out Western anti-communist ideas like fascism. On the other hand, West Berliners saw the Wall as a symbol of Soviet **repression**. From 1961 until the fall of the Wall in 1989, 171 people were killed trying to escape to West Berlin. The Wall's construction sparked off a major period of tension between the USA and the USSR.

> **repression**
> *the use of force to put down disorder and opposition*

FEAR OF WORLD WAR

Showdown at Checkpoint Charlie

As the East German guards put up the Wall, all Western troops were put on alert. There were three crossing points from one side of Berlin to the other. They were named Checkpoints Alpha, Bravo and Charlie. On October 16, 1961, US tanks were sent to Checkpoint Charlie, where they met Soviet tanks. At one point the muzzles of a US and a Soviet tank actually touched. Both the USA and the USSR prepared for possible war. This became known as the Berlin Wall crisis.

SOURCE 2 From an interview with General Anatoly Gribkov, Soviet Army High Command during the Berlin Wall crisis.

"Khrushchev ordered the commander of Soviet troops in Germany that, if the West used force, they should respond with force."

SOURCE 3 From an interview with Colonel Jim Attwood, US Military Mission in West Berlin, August 1961.

"The dead seriousness of it became more intense with each hour. The Western forces went on alert, the Strategic Air Command went on alert, NATO went on alert, troops were being made ready around the world."

Confrontation avoided

To ease the tension, US President Kennedy secretly sent a message to Premier Khrushchev. As a result, both US and Soviet troops pulled back from the Wall. Tension eased. Confrontation was avoided. Following the crisis, President Kennedy greatly increased US military spending.

Kennedy at the Berlin Wall, 1963

In 1963, Kennedy visited the Berlin Wall. In front of thousands of West Berliners he said, "We are all free when this city will be joined as one. All free men are citizens of Berlin, and as a free man I take pride in the words, 'Ich bin ein Berliner'!"

Kennedy thought the final German phrase would mean 'I am a Berliner'. What he actually said, in translation, was 'I am a jam doughnut'! The correct phrase is 'Ich bin Berliner'.

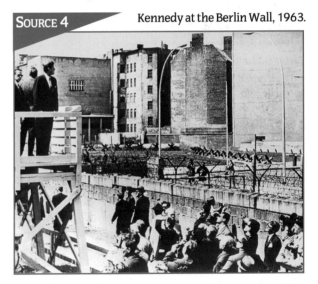

SOURCE 4 Kennedy at the Berlin Wall, 1963.

Questions

1. Why did the East Germans decide to build a wall around West Berlin in 1961?
2. Study Sources 2 and 3. How do they show that the building of the Berlin Wall caused a major crisis between the USA and USSR? Explain your answer.
3. Both US President Kennedy and Soviet Premier Khrushchev played major roles in the Berlin Wall crisis. Write down the ways each leader helped cause the crisis. Then write down ways each leader helped end the crisis. Who do you regard as more responsible for the Berlin Wall crisis: Kennedy or Khrushchev?

The Cuban Revolution, 1959

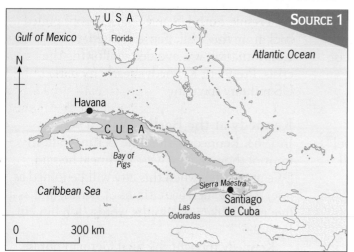

Cuba, and its proximity to the USA.

WHY WAS CUBA IMPORTANT?

Up until the late 1950s the Cold War was focused on Europe and Asia. In 1959 it was extended to Central America.

A political revolution in Cuba saw the overthrow of the dictator Fulgencio Batista. His government was replaced by a new one under Fidel Castro. Although not originally a communist, Castro became increasingly close to the USSR. The USSR supplied weapons and economic aid to Cuba. Eventually Cuba became the centre of the Cold War's most serious crisis.

Cuba is the largest island in the Caribbean. It is only 70 miles from the southern tip of the US state of Florida (see Source 1).

BATISTA

In 1933 some sergeants in the Cuban army overthrew a corrupt government led by Carlos de Cespedes. One of the sergeants was Fulgencio Batista. Eventually, in 1940, Batista was elected President of Cuba, a post he held for four years. According to the Cuban constitution, he could not be re-elected. So, Batista went into exile in Florida, and, in March 1952, led a military coup that overthrew the government of President Carlos Prio Socarras. Batista became dictator – a very US-friendly dictator. During his dictatorship, American firms were allowed special privileges in Cuba, and US Mafia ran the gambling and organised crime in the capital, Havana.

CASTRO AND THE REVOLUTION

Castro's opposition and imprisonment

When Batista seized control of Cuba in 1952, he was challenged by a lawyer called Fidel Castro. Castro claimed that Batista had violated the constitution by making himself dictator. In 1952 he organised a petition against Batista. When this failed he led an attack on the Moncada army barracks in Santiago de Cuba in July 1953. Castro was captured and imprisoned. In May 1955 Castro was released in a general **amnesty** of political prisoners. He then went into exile in Mexico and the USA for a brief period, where he planned a revolution against Batista.

> **amnesty**
> allowing prisoners to go free even though they have been convicted of a crime

> **FIDEL CASTRO (1926-)**
> Castro was a trained lawyer and became well known when he led an unsuccessful rising against Batista's dictatorship. After two years fighting, he finally overthrew Batista in 1959 and made himself Prime Minister. He held this post until 1976, when he became President – a position he still holds today. A communist leader, he has reformed Cuban agriculture, education and industry. He has strengthened ties with the USSR and China, and encouraged revolutions in Latin America, as well as liberation movements in Africa.

Rebel guerrilla warfare

On December 2, 1956, Castro and 81 companions landed in Cuba at Las Coloradas. They had only a few weapons. To attack the Batista army they used **guerrilla warfare** tactics. The rebel army was organised by Castro's friend, Che Guevara, an

> **guerrilla warfare**
> fighting that avoids pitched battles and is based on tactics like ambush and sabotage

Argentinean doctor. For the next two years they based their fighting in the Sierra Maestra mountains.

On July 12, 1957, Castro issued his unofficial programme for reform. He demanded freedom of the press and civil rights for all Cubans. This was the '12th July Movement'. It helped organise strikes and military attacks on Batista's government.

BATISTA FIGHTS BACK

On May 25, 1958, Batista tried to crush the rebels. He attacked the Sierra Maestra area with 10,000 troops. Castro's forces had only 200 rifles. In two months Batista lost 1,000 men – of whom 450 were taken prisoner. In July 1958, at the battle of El Jigue, Castro's forces won a major victory. After that victory, the rebels left the mountains and began to take towns across Cuba. By late December 1958, they were close to the capital, Havana. On January 1, 1959, Batista fled Cuba for the USA. Castro arrived in triumph in Havana a week later. He was only 33 years old when he became ruler of Cuba.

| SOURCE 2 | Fidel Castro arriving in Havana, triumphant, in January 1959. |

REVOLUTIONARY CHANGES

When Castro came to power he expelled the US Mafia from Havana. He also made changes in the economy. Cuba was heavily dependent on the production of sugar cane. Castro aimed to change this. He also introduced land reform. This led to the break-up of large farms owned by the rich.

Shortly after the Revolution, Castro was popular with the USA. He was seen as someone who would bring democracy back to Cuba. However, within a year, all that began to

change. Castro ended freedom of the press. Political opponents were imprisoned by military courts. Castro included communists in his government. Above all, Castro began making anti-American speeches. He called on other countries in Central and South America to overthrow their governments. By early 1960 Castro was seen as a growing threat to the USA and its influence in Central and South America.

FACT FILE
CASTRO'S AGRARIAN LAW REFORM
MAY 17, 1959
- All farms over 1,000 acres to be given to landless labourers
- No foreign ownership of land
- Foreign landowners given Cuban government bonds, not money, for their land

| SOURCE 3 | The views of President Castro of Cuba. |

"The Revolution promised jobs for the people. It promised honesty in government, and health programmes which had never existed before, education programmes which had never existed before."

| SOURCE 4 | From *Cuban History*, a left-wing, pro-Castro website. |

'On April 15-26, 1959, Prime Minister Castro travelled to the USA seeking to meet US President Eisenhower. He was refused and permitted only a meeting with the Vice-President, Richard Nixon. After the meeting, Nixon reported to Eisenhower that, while Castro may deny it, he was a communist.'

Questions

1. Study Source 2. How useful is it to an historian writing about the Cuban Revolution?
2. Study Source 3. How reliable is it for what took place during the Cuban Revolution?
3. Study Source 4. Does this source fully explain why the USA and Cuba became enemies after the Cuban Revolution? Give reasons to support your case.
4. What changes did the Revolution make in Cuba?

The Bays of Pigs fiasco, April 1961

THE CIA AND CUBA

When he became President, John F. Kennedy was informed of all secret activities being carried out by the Central Intelligence Agency (CIA). One of the most important projects planned was an invasion of Cuba. When Castro took power in Cuba, many Cubans fled to the USA. As he began to turn Cuba into a communist state, still more fled. These exiled Cubans looked to the US government for help.

The USA itself was anxious as well. If communism was established in Cuba, it could also spread to other parts of Central and South America. Moreover, Castro had made anti-American speeches and said that he wanted to spread revolution in the Americas.

JOHN F. KENNEDY (1917-1963)

John F. Kennedy (JFK) became the youngest ever US President at the age of 43. He was also the first Roman Catholic to be President. When he entered office in January 1961 he called his new government programme the New Frontier. In foreign affairs, he said he would oppose communism and defend any country threatened by it. He greatly increased US support for South Vietnam. His greatest triumph was in the Cuban Missile crisis. He was assassinated on November 22, 1963, in Dallas, Texas.

US attempts to get rid of Castro

The CIA felt that Castro had to be stopped. They tried many methods, including attempts to assassinate Castro. In Operation Mongoose, he was given exploding cigars and poison was put in his shoe polish! The strangest plan of all was to give Castro the hallucinatory drug LSD just before he appeared on Cuban television. The CIA hoped Castro's odd behaviour, induced by the drug, would force Cubans to oppose him! None of these plans worked.

THE BAY OF PIGS OPERATION

The CIA's most serious plan was to secretly train and arm Cuban exiles in the USA to return to Cuba and take on Castro's regime themselves. They would use guerrilla warfare to defeat Castro in the same way that Castro had defeated Batista (see p31).

When Kennedy was informed of the CIA's plan, he could have cancelled it. Instead, he supported it. So, Cuban exiles were trained in Guatemala and, in the USA, in Florida and Louisiana. The CIA called the Bay of Pigs invasion 'Operation Pluto'.

THE BAY OF PIGS INVASION

In the early morning of April 14, 1961, the invasion of Cuba began. The Bay of Pigs is on the southern coast of Cuba, 125 miles south of the capital, Havana (see Source 1, p30). 1,500 Cuban exiles landed on the beach. US B26 bombers with Cuban markings attacked Cuban soldiers.

The air attack resulted in international opposition to the attack. So, Kennedy called off further air support. This doomed the invasion.

Equipped with Soviet tanks and artillery, Castro's troops overpowered the exiles within 72 hours of the invasion. The exiles were either killed or captured. This was a great victory for Castro, and a grand humiliation for the USA.

On hearing of the failed invasion, Kennedy said, "How could I have been so stupid?" He went on US television and claimed full responsibility for the defeat.

SOURCE 4

Castro's forces repel the invasion of the Bay of Pigs by US-trained Cuban rebels.

WHAT WAS THE IMPACT OF THE BAY OF PIGS FIASCO?

In the USA

The failed invasion did not stop the USA putting pressure on Cuba. All US trade with Cuba was stopped. The USA also encouraged other countries to stop trading with Cuba. US citizens were forbidden to travel there.

In Cuba and the USSR

On the Cuban side, Castro was hailed as a great hero. He had defeated the mighty USA. The USSR also felt confident. Its leader, Khrushchev, met Kennedy in June 1961 in Vienna, after the Bay of Pigs fiasco. Khrushchev had thought Kennedy was too young and inexperienced to be a strong leader of the USA. To capitalise on this perceived weakness, in August 1961, with Soviet support, the East Germans built the Berlin Wall (see p28). This brought to a close the only break in the Iron Curtain.

Khrushchev's low opinion of Kennedy's leadership qualities was also behind the USSR's boldest move yet. In 1962 Khrushchev decided to locate Soviet nuclear missiles on Cuba. This sparked off the most serious crisis in the whole Cold War. Because of it, the world faced nuclear annihilation.

SOURCE 5

A US cartoon on the Bay of Pigs Invasion. It shows Uncle Sam puffing an exploding Cuban cigar.

Questions

1. Study Sources 1 and 2. What reasons are given in these two sources for why the USA supported an invasion of Cuba?
2. Study Source 5.
   a) What statement is this cartoon trying to make about the Bay of Pigs invasion?
   b) Do you think this cartoon gives an accurate view of what took place as a result of the failed invasion? Give reasons for your answer.
3. 'President Kennedy was responsible for the failure of the Bay of Pigs invasion.' Do you agree with this statement? Explain your answer, using information and sources from this section.

Eyeball to eyeball: the Cuban Missile crisis

CUBA AND SOVIET NUCLEAR MISSILES

For 13 days in October 1962 the world came very close to all-out nuclear war. The crisis arose when the USA discovered Soviet nuclear missile sites on Cuba. There were already a number of US nuclear missile bases on it. The Soviet missiles could reach most of continental USA (see Source B, p36). Also, the launch to impact time was so short (around 17 minutes) that it was virtually impossible for the USA to retaliate by firing nuclear missiles at either Cuba or the USSR.

SOURCE 2   A photograph of the missile sites in Cuba, taken by a US U2 spy plane in 1962.

SOURCE 1   Roger Hilsman, Head of Intelligence at the US State Department (Foreign Ministry), on what the Cuba-based missiles could have done.

'A first strike would have knocked out all the American air bases, bomber bases, all American missile bases and all American cities except Seattle in Washington State.'

In July 1962 a large number of Soviet ships began arriving in Cuba. By October, 150 had arrived. They were transporting nuclear missiles and 40,000 Soviet military advisers. The missiles were discovered by US U2 spy planes, which flew high in the atmosphere (90,000 feet; see Source 2). US President Kennedy found out about the Soviet missile sites on October 15. The crisis began.

WHY DID THE USSR PLACE NUCLEAR MISSILES ON CUBA?

The USA had missiles in Turkey
This was the first time the USSR had placed missiles outside its own borders. The USA already had Jupiter missile emplacements in Turkey, close to the USSR's southern border.

Khrushchev's opinion of JFK
Soviet Premier Khrushchev underestimated Kennedy, thinking he was weak and inexperienced. The Bay of Pigs fiasco in April 1961 had confirmed this view. When they met in Vienna in June 1961, Khrushchev tried to bully Kennedy over Berlin (see p28). The USA did not try to stop East Germany building the Berlin Wall in August 1961, so the Soviet leader took a gamble. He thought Kennedy would not stop the USSR putting missiles on Cuba, either. Khrushchev could then use the missiles to bully the USA if a crisis occurred elsewhere in the world.

NSC AND EXCOM

On October 15, 1962, Kennedy met with the National Security Council (NSC). This committee contained all the heads of the US armed forces, as well as Kennedy's top political advisers. Several NSC meetings followed. These decided what the USA would do. On October 22, the President created an even smaller group of advisers within the NSC. This was the Executive Committee of the NSC (EXCOM). All the most important US decisions in the crisis were made by these two groups. What would the USA do? (See box, p35.)

THE CRISIS UNFOLDS

The height of the crisis came from Monday 22 to Saturday 27 October, 1962.
October 22 Kennedy went live on US television. He told America that Soviet missiles had been found on Cuba. He also announced that the USA was going to blockade Cuba. Any Soviet ship going through the blockade would be searched.
October 23 The blockade began. But Soviet ships still sailed towards Cuba. Both the USA

and USSR put their armed forces on high alert. US forces went to DEFCON 2 (Defence Condition 2). (The highest type of alert in the USA is DEFCON 1 – all-out nuclear attack.) All US armed forces around the world were ready to attack the USSR if Soviet ships broke the blockade. Kennedy threatened nuclear war.

October 24 A Soviet ship went through the blockade. It was stopped and searched, but no military equipment was found.

October 26 A breakthrough. Khrushchev sent a message to Kennedy. If the USA promised not to attack Cuba and the blockade was lifted, Soviet missiles might be withdrawn.

October 27 Now, however, Khrushchev sent a tougher message, demanding removal of US missiles from Cuba. A U2 spy plane was shot down over Cuba. Fear of war reached its peak. Kennedy replied to the message of October 26, not 27. He agreed not to attack Cuba and would end the blockade if Soviet missiles were removed. The world held its breath.

October 28 US planes spotted Soviet ships turning back from the blockade line. US Secretary of State (Foreign Minister), Dean Rusk said, "We were eyeball to eyeball and the other guy just blinked."

On that day Khrushchev agreed to remove Soviet missiles from Cuba if the USA removed its missiles from Turkey. The crisis was over.

WHAT HAPPENED AFTER THE CRISIS?

Both sides realised that they had come very close to nuclear war. To improve communication, the Molink was created. This was a direct telephone link between the White House in Washington DC and the Kremlin in Moscow. In the following year, Kennedy and Khrushchev helped pass the Test Ban Treaty. They agreed to test nuclear weapons only underground. They also agreed to stop the spread of countries obtaining nuclear weapons.

SOURCE 3 A British cartoon on the Cuban Missile crisis. Khrushchev is on the left and Kennedy is on the right. They are both sitting on H-bombs.

Questions

1. *Produce a timeline of the Cuban Missile crisis. What day do you regard as the most serious in the entire crisis? Give reasons for your answer.*
2. *Study Source 2. How reliable do you think this photograph is as evidence that the USSR had placed nuclear missiles on Cuba? Explain your answer.*
3. *Study Source 3. How accurate is this cartoon in its portrayal of the Cuban Missile crisis? Give reasons to support your answer.*
4. *Who was more to blame for the Cuban Missile crisis: Kennedy or Khrushchev? Explain your answer, using information and sources from this section.*

The Cold War, 1960-63

SOURCE A The building of the Berlin Wall. From a speech made by the Prime Minister of East Germany, August 10, 1961. This speech was made three days before the building of the Berlin Wall was started.

The frontiers of our country will be protected at any cost. We will do everything to stop the criminal activity of the head-hunters, the slave-traders of Western Germany and the American spies.

SOURCE B The missile threat, 1962. From *A Map History of the Modern World*, by B.Catchpole, published in 1968.

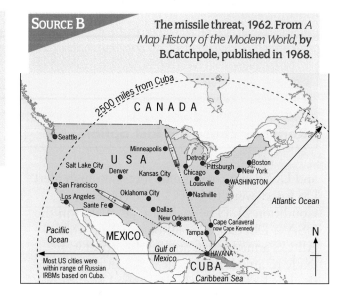

QUESTIONS AND JOHN'S ANSWERS

(a) How reliable is Source A to an historian writing about the reasons for the building of the Berlin Wall? Use Source A and your own knowledge to answer the question.
(AQA 2003)   *(6 marks)*

This source is a speech made by the East German Prime Minister. He gives reasons for the building of the Berlin Wall. Because it is by the Prime Minister of East Germany, it is an important source. The East Germans put up the Wall. The source is also from three days before the building of the Wall and gives reasons for its construction. However, it is only one person's point of view. The Prime Minister uses very strong language, such as "head-hunters" and "slave-traders". He is trying to give reasons why the Wall should be built. He doesn't mention that thousands of East Germans were fleeing to the West through Berlin. This was a much more important reason for building the Wall. Therefore, the source is deliberately biased and is unreliable in explaining the real cause for the Wall's construction.

(b) What can you learn from Source B about the dangers of missiles on Cuba to the USA?
(AQA 2003)   *(3 marks)*

Source B shows that almost all the USA could be hit by missiles from Cuba. This included big cities like Los Angeles, New York and the capital city, Washington. It also shows that missiles could not reach Seattle, Alaska or Hawaii.

(c) Describe how President Kennedy was able to obtain the withdrawal of Soviet missiles from Cuba.
(AQA 2003)   *(6 marks)*

President Kennedy was able to get the Soviets to withdraw their missiles for a number of reasons. He placed a blockade of ships around Cuba. He told the Soviets that he would not let any ships through the blockade if they were carrying weapons. The Soviets were frightened by this move because Kennedy also threatened nuclear war if the Soviets broke the blockade. This forced the USSR to remove its weapons.

(d) Did relations between the USSR and USA improve between Khrushchev coming to power in 1955, and the setting up of the Molink 'hotline' in 1963?
(AQA 2003)   *(10 marks)*

Stalin died in 1953. There was a power struggle within the USSR. By 1955 Khrushchev had become leader. In many ways relations did improve. In 1955 the USA and USSR signed the Austrian State Treaty. This meant that the four-power military occupation of Austria came to an end. Austria became a neutral country. This was a thaw in the Cold War.

However, things also got worse. In 1956 the USSR brutally put down the Hungarian Uprising. Thousands were killed. In 1957 the Soviets launched the Sputnik satellite. This started the space race between the USA and USSR, which made the Cold War worse. From 1958 to 1961, Khrushchev tried to force the Western Allies out of western Berlin. He used threats. Finally, in 1961 he ordered the East Germans to build the Berlin Wall. This caused a big freeze in the Cold War. The USA and the USSR were on the brink of war.

The worse crisis in the Cold War came in 1962, over Cuba. Khrushchev started the crisis by secretly placing nuclear missiles on Cuba. This led US President Kennedy to threaten nuclear war in order to force the missiles out of Cuba. Khrushchev agreed. So, in a way, Khrushchev helped stop a major Cold War crisis. In 1963 he also agreed to a nuclear test ban treaty and the creation of the Molink telephone hotline between Washington and Moscow.

Overall, I think relations between the USA and USSR did not improve after Khrushchev became leader, they became worse.

HOW TO SCORE FULL MARKS: WHAT THE EXAMINERS SAY

Question (a)
This question requires candidates to assess the reliability of a source.

John produces a very good answer. He deals directly with the provenance of the source. This means he identifies who wrote the source, when it was written and, most importantly of all, the motive for producing the source. To make sure that the provenance is assessed correctly, he uses his own knowledge to point out the main reason for building the Berlin Wall, not the reason the East German Prime Minister gave.

As a result, John was awarded full marks: 6 out of 6.

Question (b)
This question requires candidates to understand what is contained in a source.

John correctly mentions that the proximity of Cuba to the USA means that virtually all the continental USA could be hit by missiles fired from Cuba. But he also points out that not all the USA could be hit. Aside from the city of Seattle in the Pacific North West, he uses his own knowledge to show that two other states, Alaska and Hawaii, could not be hit.

As a result, John was awarded full marks: 3 out of 3.

Question (c)
This question requires candidates to use their own knowledge to explain a historical event.

Again John writes clearly and relevantly. He describes the events surrounding the US blockade of Cuba. However, he doesn't mention the options open to Kennedy, such as invading Cuba or using nuclear weapons. Because Kennedy chose the blockade, he gave the USSR a chance to come to an agreement. Also, John doesn't mention the US Jupiter missiles in Turkey, which bordered the USSR. One of the reasons why the USSR accepted the plan to remove its missiles from Cuba was the USA's agreement to remove its missiles from Turkey.

John gives a good description of only part of the Cuban Missile crisis. As a result, he was awarded 4 out of a possible 6 marks.

Question (d)
The question requires candidates to identify and explain causes for the change in US-Soviet relations between 1955 and 1963.

John provides many reasons why the USSR was responsible for making relations with the USA worse. He identifies the handling of the Hungarian Uprising, the Space Race, Berlin and Cuba. However, his answer is somewhat one-sided. He looks at the question only from the point of view of what the USSR did. The USA helped make matters worse by allowing West German rearmament and entry into NATO in 1955. John also fails to mention the USA's use of U2 spy planes to spy on the USSR. Eisenhower denied that U2 planes were used for spying until Khrushchev announced in 1960 that the USSR had shot one down. John could also have mentioned that US support for anti-communist forces in Laos and South Vietnam worsened relations, as well. However, he does mention important development, and gives a balanced view by pointing out that, in some ways, relations did improve.

If John had adopted a more balanced answer, covering both the USA and the USSR, he would have achieved full marks. He was awarded 7 out of a possible 10 marks.

EXTENSION WORK

'The Cuban Missile crisis proved that the USA was the stronger superpower up to 1963.' Do you agree with this statement? Explain your answer, **using information and sources from the last chapter**.

(15 marks)

• AQA accepts no responsibility whatsoever for the accuracy or method of working in the answers given.

The French War

HO CHI MINH

Vietnam had been part of the French Empire since the 1860s. It formed part of a French colony called Indo-China (Vietnam, Laos and Cambodia). In the years before the Second World War, some Vietnamese **nationalists** began to plan for the creation of an independent Vietnam. One of these was Ho Chi Minh. He had spent the early part of his adult life in Paris, France, where he had become a communist. He wanted an independent Vietnam with a system of government similar to the USSR.

> **nationalist**
> someone who wants to create an independent country, based on one language or culture

In 1940 France was defeated by Germany in the Second World War. In that year Japan forced the French government in Indo-China to let it set up military bases in that region. From 1940 to 1944, France still administered Indo-China. However, from 1944 to the end of the war in 1945, the area was under direct control of Japan.

The Viet Minh

In 1941 Ho Chi Minh helped form a pro-independence organisation called the Viet Minh. The Viet Minh received military equipment from the USA. Their troops were helped by the OSS, US special forces.

HOW DID THE FRENCH WAR START?

In August 1945, Japan was defeated in the Second World War. In September, Ho Chi Minh announced to France and the world that Vietnam was now an independent country (see Source 1). However, the Allies wanted France to be a major power after the war. Accordingly, despite Ho Chi Minh's declaration of independence, Indo-China was returned to France. France was also given a permanent seat on the UN Security Council.

Conflict between the Viet Minh and France was inevitable. In 1946 fighting broke out between them. The French War had begun. It lasted until 1954. 72,000 French were killed. This was far more than the USA lost in the American War in Vietnam between 1965 and 1973 (58,000).

SOURCE 1 The Declaration of Vietnamese Independence, September 2, 1945, by Ho Chi Minh, in Hanoi, Vietnam.

"The Declaration of the Rights of the French Revolution in 1791 states:

'All men are born free with equal rights.'

However, for more than 80 years the French have oppressed our citizens. They have founded more prisons than schools. They have robbed us of our rice fields, our forests, our raw materials. We declare to the world that Vietnam has become a free and independent country."

WHY DID THE FRENCH LOSE THE WAR?

Viet Minh guerrilla warfare

The main reason behind the French defeat was the Viet Minh's guerrilla fighting methods. They had an army of 60,000. They attacked the French troops in ambushes. They avoided set-piece battles because the French had far better military equipment and more troops (160,000).

After the Second World War, the USA withdrew its aid to the Viet Minh. Instead, it gave France military help. This was because it wanted to keep in line with Allied wishes to keep France strong. However, although the French controlled the main towns, they did not control much of the countryside. The Viet Minh had the support of the local Vietnamese population in large parts of Vietnam.

Unpopular French government

In 1949 the French tried to win support for their government in Vietnam. They installed their own Emperor of Vietnam, a Vietnamese called Bao Dai. But he received very little support from the Vietnamese people.

Defeat at Dien Bien Phu

By 1953 the French public were becoming tired of the war, and anti-war feeling developed. In that year the French tried new tactics. The French commander, General Navarre, wanted to end the war quickly. The French were given $385 million by the USA to end it. He attacked the Viet Minh in their stronghold of northwest Vietnam. A large French force was placed in the town of Dien Bien Phu. But Viet Minh soldiers surrounded it. In March 1954, after 55 days of fighting, the French force surrendered: it was a humiliating defeat.

Peace negotiations in Geneva, Switzerland ended the French War (see bottom).

(see bottom)

SOURCE 2

Adapted from *The Unfinished Journey*, by American historian William Chafe, published in 1995.

'Between 1950 and 1954, the US spent $2.6 billion in helping the French in Indo-China. The USA urged the French to give Vietnam independence. This would take support of the people away from the communist Viet Minh. Instead, the French appointed Bao Dai as ruler. He had very little support because the French still controlled Vietnam.'

SOURCE 3

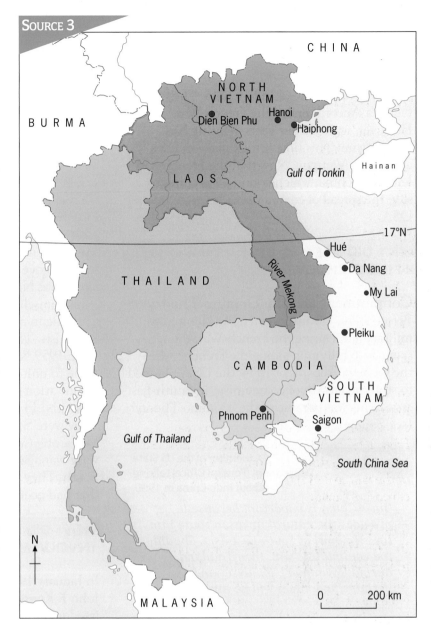

Indo-China in 1954, after the Geneva Accords.

THE GENEVA ACCORDS OF 1954

The agreement was signed by the USA, Britain, France, communist China, and the USSR.

- The French agreed to leave Indo-China
- Four new countries were created: Cambodia, Laos, North Vietnam, South Vietnam
  - Cambodia and Laos became monarchies
  - Vietnam was divided in two. North Vietnam became communist. It was ruled by Ho Chi Minh. South Vietnam became non-communist. The two Vietnams were divided by the 17°N line of latitude
- Plans were made to hold elections in North and South Vietnam to unite the country

Questions

1. Study Source 1. How useful is it as evidence of the reasons why the French War began?
2. Study Source 2. How reliable is it as evidence of why the French lost the War against the Viet Minh in 1954?
3. Study Source 3. Does the information in the map suggest that the Geneva Accords decision to divide Vietnam along the ceasefire line was fair to the Viet Minh? Explain your answer.
4. Why were the Viet Minh able to defeat the French by 1954? Explain your answer, using information and sources in this section.

The USA gets involved

In 1954 peace came to Indo-China. The Geneva Accords ended the French War. However, within a few years, fighting had begun again. This time it took place in Laos and South Vietnam. Now that the French had left Indo-China, which country was going to stop the spread of communism? It was to be the USA.

WHY DID THE USA BECOME INVOLVED IN INDO-CHINA?

Containment and the Domino Theory
Before 1954, US involvement was limited to military aid. During the French War, the USA spent $2.6 billion in aiding the French. After the Geneva Accords of 1954, the USA planned to stop the growth of communism in South-East Asia. This was because of the 'Domino Theory' (see Source 2).

Fears that communists would win the Vietnamese elections
The Geneva Accords of 1954 agreed that nationwide elections would take place in Vietnam in 1956 (see p39). The elections would decide what type of government a united Vietnam would get. However, US President Eisenhower forced South Vietnam not to hold elections in 1956 because he feared that the Viet Minh communists would win. Instead, the USA set up a government in South Vietnam. The leader was Ngo Dinh Diem, and he quickly made himself dictator. Diem was a Roman Catholic in a country where most people were Buddhists. This made his government unpopular.

In 1959 North Vietnam felt the time had come to unite Vietnam by armed force. An organisation called the National Liberation Front (NLF) was created in South Vietnam. They were South Vietnamese communists, or Viet Cong (VC) for short. The VC planned to wage war against Diem's government in the South. They would use the same guerrilla tactics that had been used against the French.

HOW DID KENNEDY INCREASE US INVOLVEMENT?

In January 1961 the USA had a new President, John F. Kennedy. He had said he would defend freedom around the world against communism (see Source 1, p32).

Laos
In 1961, Kennedy faced two communist threats in Indo-China. One was in Laos. Communist forces called the Pathet Lao were given military aid by North Vietnam. They were trying to overthrow the royal government created in 1954.

Kennedy sent military aid to the royal government. He also allowed the CIA to train a native guerrilla army to fight the Pathet Lao. The CIA ran its own private airline to provide supplies. It was called Air America and operated from Thailand. The USA also sent US bombers to attack Pathet Lao positions in central Laos. Even though war was never officially declared in Laos, by 1975 it had become the most bombed country in world history.

South Vietnam

Kennedy increased military aid to South Vietnam. He also sent military advisers to train and direct the South Vietnamese Army (known as ARVN). By the time of Kennedy's assassination in November 1963, there were 16,000 US military advisers in South Vietnam. Kennedy sent a new unit of the US army to South Vietnam – the Green Berets. They were trained in counteracting guerrilla warfare.

The USA also encouraged the South Vietnamese to use villages in strategic positions in their bid to defeat the Viet Cong. Whole villages were moved behind barbed wire and machine gun posts.

Diem's unpopularity

All this aid did not stop Diem's government from being unpopular in South Vietnam. In the spring of 1963 Buddhists across the country protested against Diem's government. As a Catholic, Diem would not allow Buddhists to celebrate Buddha's birthday. The height of the protests came when some Buddhist monks set fire to themselves in protest outside Diem's palace in Saigon, capital of South Vietnam (see Source 3).

On November 22, 1963, President Kennedy himself was assassinated. At that time South Vietnam looked on the verge of collapse. The Viet Cong controlled large parts of the countryside. Buddhists still disliked the government.

When Diem was overthrown, people began to hope matters would improve. However, there was no strong anti-communist leader to replace Diem.

A Buddhist monk committing suicide by setting himself on fire outside the Presidential Palace, Saigon, June 11, 1963. This picture appeared around the world in newspapers and on television.

SOURCE 3

THE WAR AGAINST THE VIET CONG

In early 1963, South Vietnamese forces were struggling against the Viet Cong. In January a battle took place at Ap Bac. 2,000 ARVN soldiers, supported by US helicopters and bombers, could not defeat 350 Viet Cong armed only with rifles and machine guns.

The US government decided to take action. Kennedy agreed to allow the CIA to overthrow Diem's government. This was because it was now very unpopular and losing support to the communists. The CIA would work with ARVN. On November 1, a military coup, led by ARVN, overthrew Diem. The Americans planned to arrest and imprison Diem and his advisers. Instead, they were killed by ARVN.

Questions

1. Why didn't the Geneva Accords of 1954 end fighting in Indo-China?
2. Why did the USA become more involved in Indo-China after 1954?
3. Study Sources 1 and 2. Does Source 2 fully explain the reasons for US involvement mentioned in Source 1? Give reasons for your answer.
4. 'US President John F. Kennedy did little to help prevent the spread of communism in Indo-China.' Do you agree or disagree? Write down where you think Kennedy helped try to stop the spread of communism in Indo-China. Then write down where you think he made matters worse. On balance, do you think he helped?

The American War begins: 1963-65

US President John F. Kennedy was assassinated on November 22, 1963. He was replaced by his Vice-President, Lyndon B. Johnson (LBJ). When Kennedy died, the USA had 16,000 military advisers in South Vietnam. By March 1965, the USA had decided to commit troops to Vietnam. The American War had begun.

> **LYNDON B. JOHNSON (1908-1973)**
> US President from 1963 to 1969. LBJ replaced JFK when Kennedy was assassinated in November 1963. Within the USA, he made many important social reforms to help the poor and African-Americans. Overseas, he was mainly associated with greatly increasing US support for South Vietnam. He really began the American War.

WHY DID JOHNSON INCREASE US FORCES IN SOUTH VIETNAM?

JFK's legacy
Johnson carried on where Kennedy had left off. From 1961 to 1963, Kennedy had increased US military commitments to South Vietnam. Had Kennedy lived, he might still have committed more and more troops.

South Vietnam risked collapse
Following Diem's death in November 1963, the South Vietnamese government became very unstable. By the end of 1964, South Vietnam was on the edge of collapse. Was Johnson going to allow South Vietnam to go communist or was he going to do something to help?

The Domino Theory
Johnson believed in the Domino Theory. If South Vietnam fell to communism, all South East Asia would eventually fall.

Presidential pride
Johnson also had a feeling for history. He did not want to be the first US President to lose a war.

To win votes
In 1964 Johnson faced re-election as President. His opponent was Republican candidate, Barry Goldwater. Goldwater was extremely anti-communist and accused Johnson of going soft on communism. Johnson had to show the American public that he could be tough in standing up to communism.

THE GULF OF TONKIN INCIDENT, AUGUST 1964

The most important event in forcing the US into war was the Gulf of Tonkin Incident. Johnson used it as the reason for increasing US involvement in Vietnam. Between August 2 and 4, 1964, two US destroyers were allegedly attacked by North Vietnamese torpedo boats.

The US government claimed that their ships had faced an unprovoked attack in international waters. This wasn't quite true. The Gulf of Tonkin is next to North Vietnam (see Source 3, p39). At the time of the incident, South Vietnamese military forces had been attacking the coast of North Vietnam. US destroyers were sent to cover these attacks. Naturally, the North Vietnamese saw the destroyers as aiding the South Vietnamese.

Is is also disputed whether or not the two ships were actually attacked. In 1971 Dr Daniel Ellsberg, an employee of the US Defence Department, gave secret US documents to the New York Times. Some of these documents showed that the Gulf of Tonkin Incident did not involve an actual attack by the North Vietnamese.

The Gulf of Tonkin Resolution
Johnson used the incident to get US Congress to support increased involvement in South Vietnam. By a vote of 88 to 2, the Senate (upper house of Congress) gave the President the power to send US military forces to South Vietnam. This resolution was the turning point in US involvement. It began the American War. The war lasted until 1973. It would eventually cost the lives of 58,000 US troops and approximately three million Vietnamese.

OPERATION ROLLING THUNDER

Immediately after the Gulf of Tonkin Resolution, Johnson ordered US planes to attack targets in North Vietnam. He thought that, by attacking the North, the communists might stop fighting in South Vietnam. However, in November 1964, 100 Viet Cong attacked a US air base near Saigon. Then, on February 6, 1965, Viet Cong forces attacked the US base at Pleiku.

As a result of this, Johnson decided to increase the bombing of North Vietnam. By March 1965 this had developed into a major bombing offensive, called Operation Rolling Thunder. B52 bombers (see Source 1) began bombing bridges, military bases and supply lines in North Vietnam. However, they were not allowed to bomb the capital, Hanoi, or the major seaport, Haiphong. If they did, the USA risked hitting Soviet ships, which might spark off a global war. Consequently, Haiphong remained the major supply base for Soviet and Chinese military equipment for North Vietnam and the Viet Cong.

US forces in Vietnam increased: in order to defend US air bases, 3,500 US troops were sent to Da Nang on March 8, 1965. By April 6, this had risen to 18,000.

The Ho Chi Minh trail

Between North and South Vietnam, a number of supply trails brought military supplies to the communists. These trails ran through neutral Laos. They were called the Ho Chi Minh trail. From 1965 to 1973 the US Air Force dropped thousands of bombs on the trail without successfully blocking it.

SENDING IN THE GROUND TROOPS, MARCH 1965

The US military commander in South Vietnam was General Westmoreland. He had become aware that ARVN was losing the war with the Viet Cong. US military advisers and helicopters did not seem to be making a difference. So he asked Johnson for troops.

Johnson was initially reluctant, saying, "We are not sending American boys away from home to do what Asian boys ought to be doing for themselves". Johnson's advisers were split: some supported him; others did not.

Johnson decided to start sending troops.

SOURCE 1

A US B52 'Strato-fortress' dropping bombs on targets in North Vietnam.

SOURCE 2

US President Johnson telling a friend about what he feared if he did not send troops to South Vietnam.

"Every night when I fell asleep I could hear thousands of people. They were all shouting at me 'Coward! Traitor! Weakling!' I would then wake up shaken."

SOURCE 3

The view of British historian Maldwyn Jones in *Limits of Liberty*, published in 1992. He is writing about why Johnson sent troops to Vietnam.

'Johnson believed that if the USA withdrew, no other country would feel able to rely on US promises for protection.'

Questions

1. Construct a timeline from November 22, 1963, to March 8, 1965, showing how the US increased its involvement in Vietnam.
2. Study Sources 2 and 3. They offer different reasons why US President Johnson would not withdraw support from South Vietnam.
   a) Why do they offer differing explanations?
   b) Which source do you regard as more useful in explaining why the USA would not withdraw support?
3. Why did Johnson decide to increase US involvement in Vietnam? Explain your answer, using information and sources from this section.

The American War: the military experience

The USA – one of the world's great military powers – entered the American War with high hopes of success. It was fighting the Viet Cong (VC) – an army of lightly armed, part-time, peasant soldiers. However, as the war developed, more troops from the North Vietnamese Army (NVA) became involved. These were well-trained regular soldiers. They had more advanced weapons, including Soviet-made T54 tanks.

CONDITIONS IN VIETNAM

Most fighting took place in South Vietnam, though later also in Cambodia. Throughout the war, the US used its air force to attack North Vietnam and Laos. South Vietnam is a very mountainous country, and also heavily forested. Its climate is tropical, with a high rainfall, most of which falls during the monsoon (June-August). This made normal warfare at this time very difficult.

US TACTICS

Helicopters
The USA had massive weapons and air superiority. Helicopters were used to transport troops quickly to areas of communist activity. The most widely used helicopter was the Bell Iriquois, also known as the Huey (short for Helicopter Utility).

Search and destroy
In theory, US troops were meant to search for and locate the enemy, and then use massive military superiority to destroy them. This was not easy: the enemy hid in the forest. Also, Viet Cong troops were farmers by day and soldiers by night, so they were very hard to identify, let alone find. Villages that had supported or housed communist troops were burnt and destroyed as punishment.

Chemical defoliants
To locate communist forces in forested areas, the USA used chemical defoliants to strip trees and bushes of their leaves. The most famous of these was Agent Orange. They were sprayed on the forests from planes. Besides destroying the leaves, they poisoned the water supply and killed livestock. Many innocent Vietnamese developed cancer, and children were born malformed or dead, as a result of Agent Orange.

The Phoenix Programme
The CIA tried to destroy support for the communists. They used secret agents to locate and assassinate communist supporters. Thousands disappeared and many innocent Vietnamese, mistaken as communists, were tortured or murdered.

Massive aerial bombardment
The USA relied heavily on its air superiority. Bombing raids were made on North Vietnam, Laos, and throughout South Vietnam. Tens of thousands of innocent people died. Even though the USA bombed the Ho Chi Minh trail throughout the war, they couldn't stop supplies reaching communist troops in the South. The biggest aerial bombardment of the war came in December 1972, when US bombers finally attacked Hanoi and Haiphong in North Vietnam. This was Operation Linebacker. It forced the North Vietnamese to accept a peace plan.

Allies
The USA fought the war with allies. The largest allied army was ARVN, the South Vietnamese army. This was larger than the US army in Vietnam, with approximately one million men at the height of the war.

'Winning hearts and minds'
The US created education and building programmes to show the ordinary Vietnamese that they had come to help. This aimed to win support for the American-backed South Vietnamese government.

COMMUNIST TACTICS

VC and NVA
Until 1968, most of the fighting was done by the Viet Cong. This was a volunteer army of South Vietnamese communists. The NVA (North Vietnamese Army) were regular army soldiers. They became more involved in 1968.

Guerrilla warfare

The Viet Cong used guerrilla tactics, like booby traps (see Source 1) and landmines, to harm American patrols. They also used 'hit and run' tactics – they would attack an American base or patrol and then disappear into the jungle. Many US troops said, "We rule the day but Charlie [the Viet Cong] rules the night." Because the VC could attack anywhere, at any time, it was virtually impossible to know where the front line was in the war. The VC operation was based around the Chu Chi tunnels, northeast of Saigon. In 40 square kilometres, the VC built hundreds of tunnels. These contained hospitals, sleeping accommodation, kitchens and weapons stores. The USA was never able to capture the tunnel network.

SOURCE 1

A US soldier passes a booby trap set by the Viet Cong.

SOURCE 2

The view of General Giap, Commander of the North Vietnamese Army during the American War.

"We were not strong enough to drive out half a million American troops. That was not our aim. Our aim was to break the will of the Americans to continue the war."

THE TET OFFENSIVE

Tet is the name for the Vietnamese New Year celebrations. In 1968, a ceasefire was organised for Tet. However, the VC used the ceasefire to launch a nationwide attack on ARVN and American bases. The communists hoped these attacks would start a national anti-US uprising. It was called the Tet Offensive.

At the start, the Tet Offensive had some success. VC soldiers got into the US Embassy compound in Saigon but not the embassy itself. They also captured Hué, in central Vietnam. However, after the initial shock, US and ARVN troops defeated the VC. It was a significant military defeat for the communists. From 1968, more of the war was fought by North Vietnamese Army troops (NVA).

The impact of the Tet Offensive

Although the communists had suffered a major military defeat, the real losers were the Americans. General Westmoreland had said, beforehand, that the communists were on the verge of defeat. Yet the USA was shaken by the extent of the communist attacks. It was a turning point in the American War. Afterwards, the anti-war movement grew rapidly within the USA. Attempts were made to cut down the number of US troops used in the war (see Source 3). General Westmoreland was replaced with General Creighton Abrams.

SOURCE 3

US troop levels in Vietnam, 1962-1971.

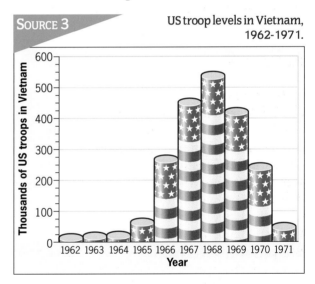

Thousands of US troops in Vietnam

Year: 1962 1963 1964 1965 1966 1967 1968 1969 1970 1971

Questions

1. Draw a spidergram showing the different tactics used by the USA during the American War.
2. Study Source 2. How useful is this source as evidence of the views of the communist forces during the American War?
3. Why was the USA unable to win the war in Vietnam between 1965 and 1973? Explain your answer, using information and sources in this section.

The American War: the civilian experience

The war in Vietnam was not like the Second World War or the Korean War. There was no front line. Fighting took place all over South Vietnam, and ordinary Vietnamese could be caught in the war at any time.

VIET CONG RAIDS, 'FREE FIRE' ZONES AND INNOCENT VILLAGERS

The Viet Cong could strike at ARVN or US forces anywhere in South Vietnam. The USA established 'free fire' zones, where US bombs could be dropped at any time, to hit potential VC targets. The war mainly took place outside large towns and cities. Most of South Vietnam's population lived in villages of brick or wooden buildings with thatched roofs. They grew rice and kept animals.

Like the Korean War, the Vietnam War was a civil war. In many parts of South Vietnam, the government changed at dusk. During the day, the pro-US South Vietnamese government ruled the village. After dark, the Viet Cong (known officially as the NLF – National Liberation Front) would arrive. Both sides demanded food and money from villagers.

The war had a terrible effect on ordinary Vietnamese. 2.5 million civilians of the population of 32 million died. The North Vietnamese Army (NVA) lost 650,000 and the Viet Cong one million. ARVN lost 750,000, while the USA lost 58,000.

THE IMPACT OF WAR

Napalm bombing

Napalm is a petroleum jelly that causes terrible burns to those affected by it. It was dropped by the USA all over South Vietnam. Napalm bombing resulted in one of the most famous photographs of the war, taken in June 1972 (see Source 1).

Cluster bombs

Cluster bombs were bombs that contained hundreds of small bomblets. They fell on villages and paddy fields, where rice was grown. Civilians and their livestock were wounded or killed by them.

Innocent villagers fleeing a napalm attack on the village of Trang Bang, June 1972.

Inflation and prostitution

At the height of the American War there were 500,000 US troops in Vietnam. They had money to spend. This caused a major rise in prices (inflation). They also brought modern goods that the Vietnamese had not seen, like radios, televisions, and fans. Tens of thousands of Vietnamese moved from villages to cities to work for the Americans or to acquire goods like these. Prostitution and drug abuse grew rapidly.

Agent Orange

The US dropped thousands of tonnes of chemical defoliant on Vietnam, destroying forests and poisoning water. They also made thousands of Vietnamese develop cancer, and give birth to dead or deformed babies.

War crimes

During the war both sides killed civilians. Many massacres took place. In the most infamous, US troops murdered the entire population of a village called My Lai (see Source 3, p39). 347 women, children and old people were killed, along with their livestock. Their village was burned. This was the My Lai Massacre of March 16, 1968. The leader of the troops in question (from Charlie Company of the 20th Infantry Division) was Lt. William Calley. He was court-martialled in 1970 and sentenced to life imprisonment in 1971 for his actions. However, in 1974, US President Nixon pardoned him. My Lai was just one of hundreds of villages that suffered in this way.

American historian Neil Sheehan writing about the My Lai Massacre.

'One soldier missed a baby lying on the ground twice with a pistol as his comrades laughed at his marksmanship. He stood over the child and fired a third time. The soldiers beat women with rifle butts. They threw dead animals into the wells to poison the water.'

SOURCE 3

Adapted from a website on the Vietnam War.

'On February 25, Charlie Company walked into a minefield. Three men died and 12 were wounded. The soldiers became demoralised because they had lost nearly 30 per cent of their soldiers in two months. When they went into My Lai on March 16 they had two aims:
1. To avenge the lives of soldiers killed in the past few months.
2. To meet the Army's 'body count'- the measurement by which army commanders in Saigon and Washington evaluated the war's progress.'

AFTER THE WAR

'Re-education' camps

The suffering of ordinary Vietnamese did not end with the fighting. When the communists finally won the war in 1975, 300,000 Vietnamese who had worked for the Southern government were sent to 're-education' camps. These were like concentration camps. Inmates suffered beatings and torture. Thousands died.

The Boat People

Many people in South Vietnam did not like the communist victory, in particular the Chinese minority who lived near Saigon. Between 1975 and 1990, one and a half million left Vietnam – many by boat. They tried to reach Malaysia, Hong Kong and Thailand, but thousands drowned in unsafe or overcrowded boats. Others were attacked by pirates. In Hong Kong the Boat People were placed in detention camps. Others were allowed to settle in the USA and Australia.

THE 'KILLING FIELDS' OF CAMBODIA

One of the worst episodes in the American War was Cambodia. In 1970 the USA and ARVN invaded Cambodia. They believed it was being used as a communist base. Thousands of bombs were dropped in the hope of killing communists. Instead, thousands of innocent Cambodians died. The USA overthrew the ruler, Prince Sihanok. He was replaced by the pro-American Lon Nol. Lon Nol's government was very unpopular and corrupt, so many Cambodians turned their support to the Khmer Rouge – Cambodian communists.

The Khmer Rouge

In 1975, when Vietnam fell to the communists, the Khmer Rouge took power in Cambodia. They wanted to create a completely new society, in which everyone was a farmer. They forced everyone living in towns and cities into the countryside. Money was abolished. Anyone with an education was arrested. Millions were forced to work in the countryside. In 1979 the Vietnamese overthrew the Khmer Rouge government of Pol Pot. They discovered that the Khmer Rouge had killed and tortured three million people out of a population of nine million to create their new society. Anyone linked to modern society (teachers, doctors, office wokers, etc.) had been murdered.

Questions

1. In what ways were ordinary Vietnamese civilians affected by the American War?
2. Study Source 1. How useful is this photograph as evidence of how ordinary Vietnamese civilians were affected by the American War?
3. Study Sources 2 and 3. These sources give different views about the My Lai Massacre.
   a) In what ways are they different?
   b) Do you think the soldiers of Charlie Company were completely to blame for the My Lai Massacre? Explain your answer.
4. What do you think was the worst effect of the American War on ordinary civilians? Explain your answer, using information and sources in this section.

Opposition at home

THE IMPACT OF WAR

The war in Vietnam divided American from American in a way unseen since the American Civil War of 1861 to 1865. Supporters of the war were called 'Hawks'. Opponents were called 'Doves'. In 1968, Richard Nixon was chosen as the Republican Party's presidential candidate. In his acceptance speech he said: "North Vietnam cannot defeat America. Only Americans can defeat America." He meant that it was opposition within the USA that would cost it victory.

WHY DID SOME AMERICANS OPPOSE THE WAR?

The draft
The USA had compulsory military service for males over 18 during the Vietnam War. This was called 'the draft'. They were expected to do a 'tour of duty' of 365 days in Vietnam. Many of these men did not want to go to war.

They felt the war was wrong
Many thought the Vietnam War was unjust. Americans were told by the government that they were defending the USA from communism. Yet Vietnam was over 12,000 miles away and it was a poor country. How could it be a threat to the USA?

Media coverage
TV coverage of the war created opposition. Pictures of US soldiers wounded or dying, villages set on fire, and innocent civilians killed appeared on the news every night. Students began demonstrating against the government. A favourite chant was: "LBJ! LBJ! How many kids did you kill today?"

The Military-Industrial Complex
Some US companies that made military vehicles and weapons were making huge profits from the war. To many Americans, this was wrong.

There was also a belief that the government had created a fear of communism simply to force the US Congress to vote taxes for the war. The idea that government and businesses both wanted a war for their own financial benefit was called the Military-Industrial Complex.

The Tet Offensive
At the end of 1967, the US military had told Americans that the war was virtually won. However, the Viet Cong Tet Offensive (see p45) of January-February 1968 showed this not to be true. It was a big turning point in US public opinion. After it, many Americans thought the war would go on for years, involving thousands of extra troops and yet more death. One of the USA's most famous TV newsmen, Walter Cronkite, visited South Vietnam just after the Tet Offensive. When he returned to the USA he claimed the war couldn't be won. This also caused a big increase in anti-war feeling.

Nixon's secret invasion of Cambodia
Opposition reached a peak in April 1970. The American people found out that President Nixon had ordered a secret invasion of Cambodia. He had not told the US Congress. Rioting occurred across the USA, mainly at

SOURCE 1

A student shot dead at Kent State University, Ohio, in 1970.

universities. During a riot at Kent State University, the University principal called in the Ohio State National Guard to restore order. The National Guards shot dead four students (see Source 1).

The Pentagon Papers

Opposition increased in 1971, when Dr Daniel Ellsberg released the 'Pentagon Papers' to the New York Times. Ellsberg worked for the Defence Department (the Pentagon). The papers were secret documents showing that the US government had lied to the US people about its involvement in Vietnam. In particular, it showed that the Gulf of Tonkin Incident of August 1964 (see p42) never actually took place.

WHAT FORM DID PROTESTS TAKE?

Public demonstrations

People demonstrated outside public buildings, like the White House. Those called for military service burnt their call-up cards in public in protest. In 1972, anti-war protestors demonstrated at the Republican Party National Convention. One was Ron Kovic. He was a solider who had been badly wounded in Vietnam and was paralysed from the waist down. His life story was made into the film *Born on the 4th of July*, starring Tom Cruise. Also in 1972, in Washington DC thousands of Vietnam veterans marched against the war. Hundreds threw away their campaign medals in protest.

Rioting

Serious rioting occurred in many towns and cities. One of the worst took place in Chicago in August 1968. Thousands of anti-war protestors went to the Democratic National Convention, where a presidential candidate to replace President Johnson was being chosen. They were protesting against pro-war candidates. Hundreds were injured as rioters fought with armed police.

Soldiers in Vietnam

By 1971, opposition had even spread to the armed forces in Vietnam. Racial tension developed between black and white troops. Drug abuse increased alarmingly. In that year, 5,000 troops were treated for combat wounds; 20,500 received treatment for drug addiction! Troops even attacked their own officers.

WHAT IMPACT DID PROTESTS HAVE?

The end of LBJ

The biggest effect of anti-war protest was to end the presidential career of Lyndon B. Johnson. In 1968, several politicians put their name forward as anti-war presidential candidates. Following the rise in support for these candidates, Johnson decided not to run for another term as President. In a speech in March 1968, he announced this decision. In the 1968 election, both Democrat and Republican candidates wanted to end the war. Democrat Hubert Humphrey wanted to negotiate a peace settlement. Republican Richard Nixon wanted 'peace with honour'.

SOURCE 2	The view of American historian Howard Zinn, adapted from *A People's History of the USA*, published in 1980.

'Vietnam gave clear evidence that the political leaders were the last to take steps to end the war. The 'people' were far ahead. The President was always far behind.'

Nixon and troop reductions

From 1968 onwards, the majority of Americans wanted the USA to leave Vietnam. When Nixon won the presidential election, he began troop reductions. However, it took until 1973 for a peace settlement to be made. The loss of support at home completely undermined the US attempt to stay in Vietnam.

In many ways, Richard Nixon was right when he said only Americans could defeat the US war effort in Vietnam.

Questions

1. *Study Source 1. How did this photograph help the anti-war movement within the USA? Explain your answer.*
2. *Study Source 2. Does this source fully explain why the USA decided to end the war in Vietnam? Give reasons to support your answer.*
3. *Why did many Americans oppose the Vietnam War? Explain your answer, using information and sources in this section.*

Peace with honour?

Throughout the American War, the USA tried to arrange a peace agreement with North Vietnam. The USA hoped that its defence of South Vietnam would force the North to stop fighting. In March 1968, President Johnson announced he would not try for re-election as President. Instead, he would try to get a peace agreement with North Vietnam. He was willing to stop bombing North Vietnam. In May 1968, the first official talks began between the USA and North Vietnam in Paris, France. Unfortunately, by the time Johnson left the White House in January 1969, no agreement had been made.

> ## SOURCE 1
> **British historian Derrick Murphy, writing about Vietnam in 2001.**
>
> 'Despite their superior technology and money, it seemed the USA could not win the war. The Americans were still backing an unpopular, corrupt government that lacked the support of the majority of the Vietnamese people.'

WHAT WAS NIXON'S 'PEACE WITH HONOUR'?

When Nixon became US President in January 1969, he said he wanted 'peace with honour' in Vietnam. This meant that the USA was willing to remove its troops without looking like it had lost the war.

Vietnamisation
In 1969, Nixon announced his 'Vietnamisation' policy. He wanted ARVN to play a much greater role in the war, and allow US troop numbers to drop. From 1969 to 1972, Nixon greatly reduced US presence in Vietnam. By 1972, the policy seemed to have worked. In March, North Vietnam invaded South Vietnam. Although the North gained control of some northern provinces, the attack was stopped by ARVN with US air support.

The 'Madman Theory' of war
Another part of Nixon's policy aimed to convince North Vietnam that he was mad, and would use nuclear weapons to win a peace agreement. An attack on a neutral country would be evidence of this. So, in 1970, US and ARVN forces invaded Cambodia. The US Air Force also bombed Laos heavily. Nixon hoped this would frighten the North into signing an agreement.

Détente
A vital method of forcing North Vietnam to agree was to befriend its allies: the USSR and communist China. North Vietnam received almost all its military equipment from these two countries. In 1971-1972, Nixon met with the Soviet leader Brezhnev. They agreed to limit their nuclear missiles. Nixon visited Moscow to sign the Strategic Arms Limitation Talks (SALT) treaty (see p60). This began a process called détente. In 1972 Nixon visited communist China. The USA finally recognised the communist government as China's official government – previously it had not. China was allowed to join the United Nations. As a result of these new, friendly relations with the communist giants, Nixon knew they would not support North Vietnam and risk upsetting the USA.

HOW WAS PEACE REACHED?

Kissinger's diplomacy
Henry Kissinger was Nixon's National Security Adviser. He negotiated with North Vietnam's representative Le Duc Tho. By October 1972, Kissinger and Le Duc Tho had created the basis for an agreement, but it was not yet signed. Both the North Vietnamese and South Vietnamese governments had to support this agreement.

Operation Linebacker I and II
Finally, to force the North to agree, Nixon began the most intense bombardment of the entire war. Starting on December 18, 1972, B52 bombers launched the Operation Linebacker I and II offensives against the North.

Nguyen Van Thieu
Thieu was President of South Vietnam.

He refused to sign any agreement that allowed communist troops to stay there. This obstructed US peace plans. To convince Thieu, Nixon told him in private that, if the communists attacked, "You can count on us". Nixon never told the US Congress this.

An American cartoon showing Kissinger, Nixon and South Vietnamese President Thieu.

"They still want us to lose a little face, namely his ... "

The Peace Agreement

On January 27, 1973, the American War came to an end. The peace agreement was accepted. Kissinger and Le Duc Tho were given the Nobel Peace Prize for their efforts.

DECISIONS MADE FOR PEACE IN VIETNAM, OCTOBER 1972

- A ceasefire in South Vietnam, Laos and Cambodia

- US forces would leave South Vietnam within 60 days of signing the agreement

- All US prisoners of war in Vietnam would be released

- North Vietnamese forces were allowed to stay in South Vietnam

THE END OF THE VIETNAM WAR

Nixon's resignation

By 1975 the situation had changed considerably. In August 1974, Nixon became the only US President to resign while in office, following Congress's investigation into his use of illegal tactics in the 1972 presidential election. This was called the Watergate Scandal. During the investigation, it was also discovered that Nixon had secretly invaded Cambodia, without Congress's support. Congress passed an act to prevent this happening again, and cut US aid to South Vietnam.

The opinion of historian Paul Kennedy, in 1988.

'The military problem [for the USA in Vietnam] was linked to a political problem. The North Vietnamese and Viet Cong were fighting for what they believed in. The independence of their country.'

The fall of South Vietnam and final withdrawal of US presence

Although it had failed in 1972, in March 1975 the North again invaded the South. Thieu asked for US military aid. Nixon had promised help, but Congress refused. Within weeks most of South Vietnam was overrun. ARVN disintegrated. Communist troops reached the outskirts of Saigon.

On April 30, 1975, a North Vietnamese T54 tank entered the Presidential Palace in Saigon. US helicopters took the last Americans away from Saigon from the roof of the US Embassy. The Vietnam War was over; North and South were united under one, communist government. The Domino Theory began to work: also in April, communists took control of Cambodia and Laos. All of Indo-China was now communist. The USA had lost a foreign war for the first time.

Questions

1. How was President Nixon able to get a peace agreement to end the war?
2. Study Sources 1 and 3. These sources give different reasons for the defeat of the USA in Vietnam.
   a) Do they fully explain why the USA lost? Explain your answer.
   b) Which source offers the better explanation for US defeat? Explain your answer.
3. Study Source 2. What statement is this cartoon trying to make about Nixon and his attempt to get a peace agreement in Vietnam?
4. Do you think Nixon achieved 'peace with honour' in Vietnam? Explain your answer, using information and sources in this section.

Vietnam since 1939

SOURCE A My Lai massacre, 1968. From an American history book, published in 1990, describing the fighting in the Vietnam War.

'The US soldiers were bewildered and afraid. The Viet Cong had surprised and ambushed them before. Now, alone in the jungle, they became panic stricken and turned on My Lai.'

QUESTIONS AND ADELE'S ANSWERS

(a) Why did the French leave Vietnam in 1954?
(AQA 2003)   *(6 marks)*

> The French left Vietnam in 1954 for a number of reasons. The most important was their defeat at the Battle of Dien Bien Phu. This was a battle in North Vietnam. The French army had been surrounded by the Viet Minh. The Viet Minh forced the French to surrender. This was a humiliation for the French. They felt that they had lost so many men since the beginning of the French War in 1946 that they should leave. During the war the Viet Minh had used guerrilla warfare tactics. They attacked French bases all over Vietnam. The French found it hard to stop them. That is also why the French decided they could not win and left.

(b) Sources A and B give different views of why the My Lai massacre took place. Why do you think they are different?
(AQA 2003)   *(8 marks)*

> Source A suggests that the US soldiers were afraid. They had been attacked many times by the VC. They felt so afraid that they decided to attack the village of My Lai.
>
> Source B gives a different story. Lieutenant Calley says that he was fighting communism. He thought that My Lai contained communists. That is why he had them killed. The sources are different because Source B is by Lieutenant Calley. He was at My Lai. He was speaking at an enquiry. He is trying to justify himself. He was facing the accusation that he had murdered innocent people. Source A is different. It is from an American history book. This book is more likely to be trying to give the reasons for the massacre, without trying to cover up.

SOURCE B From Lieutenant Calley's account of the My Lai massacre. He gave his account at the enquiry of 1969. He was later found guilty of the murder of 22 civilians and sentenced to 20 years hard labour.

"The only crime I have committed is to do with the judgement of my values. Apparently, I valued my troops more than I did that of the enemy. We were not in My Lai to kill human beings really. I was there to destroy an idea, to destroy communism."

SOURCE C Student protests against the war in Vietnam. Photograph of a student killed in anti-war demonstrations at Kent State University, USA, in 1970.

(c) How reliable is Source C to an historian studying the effects of TV and media coverage on the peace movement in America? Use Source C and your own knowledge in your answer.
(AQA 2003)   *(7 marks)*

> Source C shows a student killed at Kent State University in 1970. The students were protesting against the war. They were shot by American soldiers. The source is reliable in that it shows a real event. This picture shocked Americans.
>
> However, it is only one event. To prove that it was reliable you would have to find out what happened at other universities. In fact, this was an isolated incident. So the source is not completely reliable.

(d) Explain why the war continued to have an effect on the Vietnamese people for a long time after the fighting had stopped.
(AQA 2003)   *(8 marks)*

Even after the war came to an end, Vietnamese people suffered. Many people had been wounded in the war. They continued to suffer after the fighting came to an end. Lots of Vietnamese were affected by Agent Orange. This was a chemical that poisoned fields and rivers. It destroyed whole forests. People who ate food from Agent Orange areas developed diseases like cancer. Babies were born deformed. This went on for years after the war.

Many people who supported the South Vietnam government were put in re-education camps. These were like concentration camps. People were tortured and thousands died. Hundreds of thousands of Vietnamese wanted to leave Vietnam. They became the Boat People. They tried to go by boat to Hong Kong and Malaysia. Thousands drowned or were attacked by pirates in the attempt. Moreover, the country had been badly damaged by war. Bridges and roads were destroyed. Towns were flattened. It took years to put these things right.

HOW TO SCORE FULL MARKS: WHAT THE EXAMINERS SAY

Question (a)
This question requires candidates to explain the causes of a historical event.

Adele includes a lot of relevant information. She identifies different reasons for the French decision to leave Vietnam. She mentions the defeat at Dien Bien Phu. This had a major impact on the Geneva talks on Indo-China in 1954. She also mentions the type of tactic used by the Viet Minh. Their guerrilla warfare tactics made it very difficult for the French to find and defeat the Viet Minh. However, she neglects to mention the growth of opposition to the war within France.

Adele has developed a multi-causal answer. She finds links between her causes and places them in order of priority. As a result, she was awarded 5 out of a possible 6 marks.

Question (b)
This question requires candidates to explain why there are different interpretations of historical events, and to use their own knowledge to explain why these accounts might be different.

Adele shows in what ways the sources are different in their accounts of the massacre. She also explains why these accounts might be different. This is very important. She is able to provide motives behind each source. Lieutenant Calley was at My Lai as an officer. He gave the orders to kill the villagers. Therefore, he was trying to defend his actions when he was answering the questions of the enquiry into the massacre. However, Adele should have linked her comments to the American people's reaction to the massacre. This would have meant pointing out that the massacre was an important factor in the growth of the anti-war movement

As a result, Adele was awarded 6 out of a possible 8 marks.

Question (c)
This question requires candidates to test the reliability of a source.

Adele's answer mentions that the shootings at Kent State University in 1970 were a real event. However, she also makes an important statement about testing reliability. To prove that this type of photograph was typical in affecting the growth of the peace movement in the USA, you would have to look at other types of information from the media that covered it. She should have mentioned other aspects of the peace movement and how these were covered in the media. These would have included information about what happened within Vietnam – for example the massive bombing campaigns, the burning villages, the My Lai Massacre, and other demonstrations within the USA.

As a result, Adele was awarded 4 out of a possible 7 marks. To gain higher marks she needed to use her own knowledge in a more detailed way.

Question (d)
This question requires candidates to identify several consequences of the war in Vietnam and to find links between them.

This is a well-structured answer. Adele is able to produce a wide range of factors that directly link to the question. The material damage to Vietnam is mentioned. She also mentions more long-term factors such as the Boat People and the longer-term impact of Agent Orange. She provides an answer that identifies many consequences of the war. However, she does not gain full marks because she needed to provide a reasoned judgement at the end of her answer, summing up the points she makes about the immediate, short-term and longer-term consequences of the war.

As a result, Adele was awarded 6 out of a possible 8 marks.

EXTENSION WORK

Why did the USA leave Vietnam in 1973? Explain your answer, **using sources and information from the last chapter**.

(15 marks)

• AQA accepts no responsibility whatsoever for the accuracy or method of working in the answers given.

The Prague Spring, 1968

In 1959, Soviet Premier Khrushchev claimed that the USSR's communist government and economy would make it and its communist allies richer than the USA and the West. In fact, all was not well in the Soviet bloc. The standard of living of people in the USSR and Eastern Europe was much lower than in the USA and Western Europe. People also had very few political rights. The communist country showing most discontent was Czechoslovakia.

WHY WERE THERE REFORMS IN CZECHOSLOVAKIA IN 1968?

Czechoslovakia had been the only democratic country in Central Europe in the 1930s. It was the last country in the Soviet bloc to become communist, in 1948. By the early 1960s, Czechoslovakians were upset at poor living and working conditions, and government corruption.

In January 1968, Alexander Dubcek replaced the pro-Soviet Antonin Novotny as head of the Czechoslovak Communist Party. Then, in March, Novotny was replaced as President of Czechoslovakia by Ludvik Svodoba, a Dubcek supporter.

Dubcek wanted to introduce a more open communist society. During the spring of 1968, he introduced reforms which seemed to offer a way forward for other communist countries in Eastern Europe. These reforms were called 'socialism with a human face' (communist countries called themselves socialist).

WHAT REFORMS WERE MADE?

Censorship
A very important change was the relaxation of censorship. The government could now be criticised in the media. This had never happened before in a communist country. Soon newspapers began producing evidence that the old Novotny government had been corrupt and inefficient. Even the Communist Party criticised the former government. In April 1968, Dubcek's Communist Party complained that Novotny's government had a poor record on housing, transport and living standards. It announced it was going to make further major changes.

Business
Businesses were given greater control over their operation. Up to spring 1968, Czechoslovakia's communist government controlled what companies produced, and how much.

Workers' councils
Workers in factories were allowed to elect workers' councils. These had the right to bargain with factory managers for better pay and working conditions, just like trade unions in the West.

Foreign travel
Czechs were given the opportunity to travel freely abroad. This had never been allowed in communist countries.

New parliament
Dubcek also said a new parliament would be elected. In the elections, Communist Party members no longer had to follow the Party's views.

These reforms added up to a revolution, known as the Prague Spring. It greatly alarmed the Soviet leaders. In 1968 the USSR had joint leaders: Leonid Brezhnev and Alexander Kosygin. They had replaced Nikita Khrushchev in 1964. In May 1968, Kosygin visited Czechoslovakia. He was not happy with what he saw. On his return to Moscow (the Soviet capital), he reported that the USSR would lose power across Eastern Europe if these reforms continued.

WHAT DID THE USSR DO?

Armed manoeuvres
In June, Warsaw Pact armed forces held manoeuvres in Czechoslovakia. This was a threat to Dubcek to stop making reforms. It had no effect. In July, Brezhnev, Kosygin and the entire Soviet cabinet (Politburo) visited Czechoslovakia. The Soviets made many demands. They wanted the government to bring back censorship of the media. Even though the Dubcek government was willing to make some concessions, the Soviet government had decided to act.

Warsaw Pact tanks roll into Prague during the invasion of Czechoslovakia in August 1968.

SOURCE 2   Eduard Goldstucker, a Czech writer, talking about the Soviet invasion of Czechoslovakia in August 1968.

"I went through the Hitler invasion of 1939, and the Soviet invasion of '68 was worse. Hitler was our enemy. But the Soviets had said for decades they were our best friends and our brothers. They came with an army of half a million to suppress our attempt at more freedom. They came to crush it."

The invasion of Czechoslovakia

On the night of August 20-21, Warsaw Pact forces entered Czechoslovakia. They were told that they had been invited by loyal Czech communists to stop revolution. These troops soon realised that no anti-communist revolution had taken place. Instead of being met by cheering crowds, the troops were met by demonstrations of opposition. 150,000 Czechs and Slovaks fled the country to the West. One Czech student, Jan Palach, set fire to himself in central Prague (the capital) in protest.

The removal of Dubcek

Dubcek and his supporters were taken to Moscow for 'talks'. On August 28 Dubcek signed an agreement allowing Soviet troops to occupy Czechoslovakia on a temporary basis. Dubcek and his supporters were removed from government. For the next 20 years, until 1989, Dubcek played no part in Czech politics.

THE BREZHNEV DOCTRINE

In August 1968, Leonid Brezhnev made a very important speech. He said that, if any communist government tried to make Western-style reforms, it was up to other communist governments to stop them. This doctrine was the justification for the invasion of 1968. It also explained (in retrospect) why the USSR had invaded Hungary in 1956.

SOURCE 3   A Czech cartoon of 1968. It shows a Soviet soldier with a girl (representing Czechoslovakia) in 1945 and again in 1968. In 1945 the Soviet army 'liberated' Czechoslovakia from Nazi occupation.

Questions

1. Study Source 1. How reliable is this photograph as evidence of the Soviet invasion of 1968?
2. Study Source 2. How useful is this source as evidence of Czech reaction to the Soviet invasion of 1968?
3. Study Source 3. What statement is this cartoon trying to make about the Soviet Army and Czechoslovakia in 1945 and 1968?
4. What changes did Dubcek's government make in Czechoslovakia in 1968?
5. Why did the Soviet government dislike Dubcek's reforms? Explain your answer, using information and sources from this section.

The communist world splits: the USSR and China

In 1945 the centre of the communist world was the USSR. The USA believed that all communist groups in the world took their orders from Moscow. This view was supported by the creation of Cominform in 1947 (see p12).

There were signs early in the Cold War that this was not true. In 1945, Yugoslavia had been freed from Nazi occupation by a communist army – the Partisans (Yugoslav communists), led by Josip Tito. In 1948, Tito refused to follow orders from Moscow. Yugoslavia was forced to leave Cominform. From 1948 until the end of the Cold War, Yugoslavia was a communist country, but free from Soviet influence.

THE CHINESE REVOLUTION, 1949

A big change occurred in the communist world in 1949. China, the most heavily populated country on earth, became communist. In 1949 the Communists under Mao Zedong defeated the Nationalists in the four-year Chinese Civil War. The Nationalists then set up their own country on the island of Formosa (Taiwan), which they called the Republic of China. To highlight the difference between the two groups, communist China became the People's Republic of China.

Mao established his own, non-Soviet form of communism in China after 1949. However, he still remained friends with the USSR while Stalin ruled it. In 1950, Mao allowed Chinese communist volunteers to help the North Koreans in the Korean War (see p23).

THE USSR AND CHINA START TO SPLIT

Khrushchev and Mao
The first major split took place in 1956. In that year Soviet leader Khrushchev denounced Stalin at the Soviet Communist Congress. Mao saw this as an attack on his own form of leadership, which was similar to Stalin's. Also, after Stalin's death, Mao saw himself as the leader of world communism.

In 1956 Premier Khrushchev visited Mao in China. Khrushchev had just visited the USA. The meeting with Mao went badly. The two communist leaders disliked each other. Mao called Khrushchev "an American stooge". This meant Mao thought he was becoming too friendly with the USA.

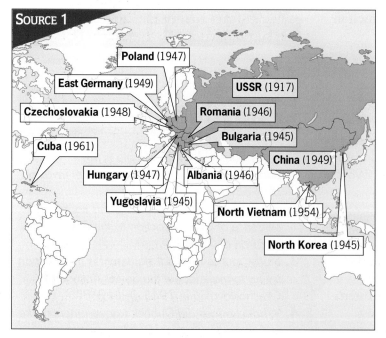

SOURCE 1

Poland (1947)
East Germany (1949)
USSR (1917)
Czechoslovakia (1948)
Romania (1946)
Bulgaria (1945)
Cuba (1961)
China (1949)
Hungary (1947)
Albania (1946)
Yugoslavia (1945)
North Vietnam (1954)
North Korea (1945)

The communist world in 1975, showing when each country became communist.

SOURCE 2
From an interview with Lev Deluisin, Soviet Ambassador to China, about the meeting of Khrushchev and Mao in 1958.

"Here were two dictators, each used to getting his own way. They couldn't co-operate. In the communist camp the question was 'Who was number one?'"

The Great Leap Forward
In 1958, Mao began the 'Great Leap Forward'. This was a plan to make communist China a rich country. The government took over all land. By 1961, the Great Leap Forward was a disaster. An estimated 30 million had starved to death. Communist China became a closed society, completely cut off from the rest of the world.

The Cultural Revolution

In 1966 Mao started the Chinese Cultural Revolution. Using enthusiastic young communists known as Red Guards, he attacked the old communist leadership. Thousands of senior communist officials were removed from office. Many were imprisoned, thousands killed. While the USSR was trying to ease tension with the USA and the West, China was becoming more extremist and anti-Western.

CHINA'S CONFLICT WITH THE USA

The first major clash between the two powers came in the Korean War. Communist Chinese volunteers fought US and UN troops. In 1954, Mao threatened to invade Taiwan. The USA threatened China with nuclear attack if it did so. In addition, in the 1960s the USA thought China was giving aid and support to North Vietnam. All these events ensured that relations between the USA and China were very tense from 1949 to 1970.

SOURCE 3
Adapted from an interview with George Elsey, an adviser to US President Truman in 1950. He is talking about the period of the Korean War, 1950-1953.

"At that time we believed Moscow and the Chinese Communists were tightly linked, hand in hand. This was seen as part of a worldwide conspiracy."

CHINA'S CONFLICT WITH THE USSR

On March 2, 1969, Soviet and Chinese military units clashed on an island in the Ussuri River, part of the border between the USSR and China. For a short period it seemed that the USSR and China might go to war. After a small-scale start, by the end of 1970 the USSR had sent approximately 250,000 troops to the Soviet-Chinese border in eastern Siberia.

However, there were other reasons for the confrontation. In the 1860s the Russian Empire had taken the area of eastern Siberia from the Chinese, who regarded it as part of their national territory. Nationalism and communism both played their part in creating the split between the two communist giants. China also saw its brand of communism as the only true type, and claimed the Soviets were 'revisionists', going soft on communism.

SOVIET-CHINESE RIVALRY

The rivalry between the USSR and China spread across the world. In 1968, Albania decided to split from the Soviet bloc, and became an ally of China. Albania became cut off from virtually every country on earth except China. Chinese was the only language taught in Albanian schools!

The most serious clash between the USSR and China came over Cambodia. In 1975 Cambodia was taken over by the communist Khmer Rouge (see p47). They were led by Pol Pot, a supporter of China. Between 1975 and 1978, Pol Pot attempted to set up an extreme version of Chinese communism. One third (three million) of Cambodians were killed or starved to death. In 1978 the Vietnamese invaded and occupied Cambodia. Vietnam was allied to the USSR. A civil war then took place in Cambodia between the two sides. In 1979, China and Vietnam fought a short but bloody border war.

All these events ensured that relations between the USSR and China remained very tense. By 1972, both countries had taken the dramatic step of making friends with their great enemy, the USA. In 1972, the USSR began the period of détente with the USA. Also, US President Nixon visited China in that year. For the first time the USA accepted the communist government in China. China was then allowed to join the United Nations.

INVESTIGATE...
Why did Mao oppose Khrushchev and Soviet communism after Stalin's death?
Go to www.spartacus.schoolnet.co.uk/ColdWar.htm

Questions

1. Study Source 1. How did communism spread throughout the world from 1945 to 1962?
2. Study Source 3. Does this source fully explain why the USA feared and disliked communism? Give reasons for your answer.
3. How did the USSR and China come into conflict after 1958? Explain your answer, using information and sources from this section.

The big thaw: détente, 1969-72

WHAT WAS DÉTENTE?

Détente is a French word. It means release from tension. It describes a new period in the Cold War that began in 1969 and reached its most important point in 1972. That year was also a major turning point in the Cold War.

NIXON VISITS THE USSR AND CHINA

In 1972 US President Nixon visited the USSR to meet Soviet Premier Brezhnev. Nixon was the first US President to do this. In 1973 Brezhnev visited the USA. These meetings helped to ease tension between the two superpowers. The long years of nuclear confrontation and fear of imminent war seemed to be over. Also in 1972, Nixon became the first US President to visit communist China, where he met Mao Zedong. As a result of that visit, the USA recognised Mao's government as the official government of China, even though Mao had been in power since 1949. China was also allowed to join the United Nations.

Why had such a major change taken place?

SOURCE 1   Nixon and Brezhnev in the USSR, 1972.

WHY DID THE USA WANT DÉTENTE?

The cost of the Cold War
The USA was looking for new ways of containing communism. The arms race was costing billions of US dollars. This expense was added to by the cost of the Vietnam War (1965-1973). In 1969 Nixon had already begun US troop withdrawals from South Vietnam. These mounting costs were affecting the US economy.

Prices began to rise (inflation). The value of the US dollar against other currencies was threatened.

Mutually Assured Destruction
The USA was also fearful of M.A.D. Both sides had so many nuclear weapons that an attack by one on the other would automatically lead to the destruction of both superpowers, and probably the entire world.

Nixon
Nixon had only narrowly won the presidential election in 1968. He wanted to be re-elected by a large majority in 1972. One way of achieving this was to ease world tension.

WHY DID THE USSR WANT DÉTENTE?

The cost of the Cold War
Like the USA, the USSR had economic problems. It was spending billions of dollars on military equipment in the arms race. This meant that living standards in the USSR were poor. Food shortages and poor housing were major problems. To increase wealth within the USSR, Brezhnev wanted to increase trade between the USSR and the West. This would reverse the policy followed by Soviet leaders since 1945.

Relations with China
Also, the USSR was frightened by the tension between itself and China since 1969. It would have been very difficult for the USSR to be the enemy of the USA and China at the same time. Something had to be done to ease tension with the USA as long as problems with China continued.

WHY DID CHINA WANT DÉTENTE?

Although détente usually refers to relations between the USA and the USSR, China also wanted to see tension eased. Like the USSR, China was fearful of isolation. Although it had nuclear weapons, the number was tiny compared to the USA and the USSR.

A US cartoon from June 3, 1972. It shows President Nixon visiting communist China, surrounded by doves of peace. On the right are Mao Zedong and Chou Enlai, leaders of communist China. The words at the bottom of the cartoon are spoken by Chou to Mao.

"It's going to be a long week..."

SOURCE 3 From an interview with Georgi Arbatov, adviser to Brezhnev.

"Brezhnev was a sincere person. He had been through the Second World War. He believed he had to do his best to prevent war."'

KISSINGER AND DÉTENTE

In 1969 Henry Kissinger was appointed National Security Adviser to President Nixon. He became the key figure, along with the President, in deciding US foreign policy. Kissinger believed in secret diplomacy. This meant he had secret talks with leaders of the USSR and China before official talks were announced. He believed that peace and stability were needed in the world – although parts of the world were communist, the USA had to accept this. On the Soviet side, the main link to Kissinger was Anatoly Dobrynin, Soviet Ambassador to the USA. Both these men met privately and secretly on a regular basis from 1969 to 1972. They laid the foundations for détente.

GERMANY AND OSTPOLITIK

Tension was also eased in Germany. In 1970 Willy Brandt became the first West German Chancellor (Prime Minister) to visit East Germany. Brandt's policy of trying to improve relations between East and West Germany was called Ostpolitik. Brandt also visited the USSR and Poland. He tried to prove to Germany's old enemies of the

Ostpolitik
German for
'Eastern policy'

Second World War that West Germany was not a country to fear. West Germany recognised for the first time the new border between Poland and East Germany (the Oder-Neisse Line). Equally, in 1972, West Germany signed the Basic Treaty, in which it recognised the existence of East Germany for the first time. Both the USA and USSR accepted the treaty. The following year, in September 1973, East and West Germany were allowed to join the United Nations.

WHAT FORMS DID DÉTENTE TAKE?

- Reduction in the number of nuclear weapons held by the USA and USSR
- Better trade between the USSR and the West
- Cultural links between the USSR and the West, including the visits of sports teams and music, dance and art groups across the Iron Curtain
- US and Soviet co-operation in space exploration

SOURCE 4 Adapted from a speech by US President Nixon to the US Congress, June 1, 1972. He is talking about détente with the USSR.

"We took the first step towards a new era. We have begun to check the wasteful and dangerous growth of nuclear weapons. We have begun to reduce the level of fear by reducing the causes of fear."

Questions

1. Why did the USA wanted to ease tension with the USSR from 1969? Explain your answer.
2. Study Source 2. How useful is this cartoon to an historian writing about détente?
3. Study Sources 3 and 4. These sources give different reasons for détente.
   a) Why do they offer different views?
   b) Which source do you think is more reliable? Give reasons for your answer.
4. Who do you think was most responsible for détente: Richard Nixon, Leonid Brezhnev, or Henry Kissinger? Explain your answer, using information and sources in this section.

Détente in action

Some forms of détente were successful, some were not.

Did it really make the world a safer place?

SALT, 1972

One of the most important parts of détente was the Strategic Arms Limitation Talks (SALT) treaty. Strategic arms are nuclear weapons. Secret talks to limit the number of nuclear weapons had begun in 1969, when Richard Nixon had become US President. Both countries were spending billions of dollars on weapons they could never use because of Mutually Assured Destruction (M.A.D.).

How far had the arms race gone?

By 1969 Nixon was facing pressure from his military commanders to increase the USA's nuclear weapon stocks. This was due in part to the development of MIRV (Multiple Independently-Targeted Re-entry Vehicle). This was a missile with more than one nuclear warhead. Each warhead could hit a different target. By 1972, on top of its 1,550 ICBMs, the USSR had 5,700 MIRV warheads. Additionally, there were ABMs (Anti-Ballistic Missiles). These were developed by both sides to intercept incoming ICBMs. They created more tension between the superpowers because each side feared they might encourage a nuclear attack on the other with no warning.

FACT FILE

THE US-SOVIET ARMS RACE, 1964 AND 1972

	USA	USSR
1964		
ICBMs	834	200
SLBMs	416	120
Nuclear Submarines	34	21
1972		
ICBMs	1,054	1,550
SLBMs	656	720
Nuclear Submarines	41	42

- ICBMs (Inter-Continental Ballistic Missiles) could hit the USA or USSR from the other superpower
- SLBMs (Submarine-Launched Ballistic Missiles) could be launched from the sea very near the other superpower, reducing reaction time

THE TERMS OF THE SALT I TREATY

Nixon and Brezhnev signed this in Moscow on May 29, 1972. It was agreed that each side's number of ICBMs should stay the same for five years. This gave the USSR more ICBMs than the USA. However, the USA had more MIRVs than the USSR. Both sides agreed to limit the number of ABMs.

SALT I was important because it was the first time that the USA and USSR had agreed to limit their nuclear weapons. However, further SALT talks between the USA and USSR stopped in 1974. This was in part due to the Watergate Crisis (see p51) in the USA, which led to the resignation of Nixon in August 1974. It was also due to US opposition to Soviet treatment of Jews within the USSR.

Salt II

When Jimmy Carter became US President in 1977, he started SALT talks again. A second SALT treaty was signed in Vienna, Austria, in 1979. This attempted to limit nuclear weapons even further. However, the US Congress did not agree to it. This was due to the Soviet invasion of Afghanistan in December 1979 (see p62).

OTHER EXAMPLES OF DÉTENTE

- In November 1971 the USA agreed to sell the USSR $136 million of wheat and $125 million in oil drilling equipment

- Premier Brezhnev helped force North Vietnam to negotiate an end to the Vietnam War. A peace agreement between the USA and North Vietnam was finally agreed in January 1973

- In 1970 U2 spy planes noticed that the USSR had built a submarine base in Cuba. Rather than see another major crisis over Cuba, both superpowers decided to end the crisis secretly

- In 1974 a US Apollo space module docked with the Soviet Soyuz Space Station

"When we went to the USA for training we met the Americans. One of them said to me: 'Since this project, I sleep better at night. I am no longer afraid of nuclear war, because we are working together.'"

détente is... ...the exchange of sweet nothings

détente is... ...covering up his treaty violations

détente is... ...knowing when to give something for nothing

SALT   HELSINKI

PROBLEMS WITH DÉTENTE

A big obstacle to détente was the issue of human rights. People in the West were upset that there was no freedom of speech or religion in the USSR or communist Central and Eastern Europe. In 1974, US Senator Henry Jackson tried to halt links with the USSR. He complained about the lack of human rights there.

Helsinki Conference, 1975

In 1975 the USA and USSR, with Canada and the major European powers (35 countries in all), signed an agreement in Helsinki. This agreement finally recognised the borders created after the Second World War (see p11). The most controversial part of the agreement involved human rights. It declared that all countries signing it should respect the human rights of their citizens, including freedom of speech. After the signing of the agreement, people in Eastern Europe complained that it had not been actively applied. In 1977 a group called Charter 77 was created in Eastern Europe. It attempted to check on human rights in communist Europe. Several of the organisers were arrested and imprisoned. For people who had hoped for greater freedom, the Helsinki Conference proved a great disappointment.

In December 1979 the USSR invaded Afghanistan. This brought détente to an end.

"The leading members of the Soviet Communist Party read the agreement. When they read the part on human rights their hair stood on end. One said it was a complete betrayal of communism. The Foreign Minister, Gromyko, said the main part of the agreement was about borders, not human rights. As for human rights, he said, 'Who is the master of the house? We are the masters. It is up to us how to act. Who can force us?'"

Questions

1. What was the purpose of the Strategic Arms Limitation Talks and treaty?
2. Study Source 1. Does this cartoon fully explain the reasons for SALT? Explain your answer.
3. Study Source 3. What statement is this cartoon trying to make about détente?
4. Study Source 4. How useful is this source to an historian writing about the Helsinki agreements of 1975?
5. In what ways was détente a success, and in what ways was it a failure? Draw a table, with two columns, to set out its successes and failures. Overall, do you think détente was a success or failure? Explain your answer, using information and sources in this section.

The Soviet invasion of Afghanistan, 1979

On Christmas Eve, 1979, US President Carter telephoned Soviet Premier Brezhnev. US spy satellites had detected Soviet military activity on its border with Afghanistan. Carter asked Brezhnev if the USSR planned to invade Afghanistan. Brezhnev said no. The next day Soviet troops invaded and occupied Afghanistan. Détente was shattered. A new Cold War had begun.

WHY DID THE USSR INVADE AFGHANISTAN?

History
Central Asia had been important to the old Russian Empire since the 1860s. By the 1880s this Empire bordered Afghanistan, as did the British Empire from the south. This led to a confrontation between the Russian and British Empires. Both countries wanted to control Afghanistan. This rivalry continued until after the First World War. Even in the 1960s and 1970s, the USSR wanted influence in Afghanistan. So, by invading and occupying the country in 1979, the USSR was completing a Russian plan over 100 years old.

Fear of Islam
The USSR feared the influence of Islam. In January 1979, a radical Muslim government was established in Iran. US Embassy staff were arrested and held hostage.

All Soviet Central Asia was Muslim, and the USSR feared that radical Islam would spread from Iran into the heart of its communist, atheistic territory. In order to stop this from happening, it occupied Afghanistan.

Soviet Central Asia
an area now divided into Uzbekistan, Kazakhstan, Turkmenistan, Krygyzstan and Tajikistan - countries created after the collapse of the USSR in 1991

Civil war in Afghanistan
In 1978, the pro-Soviet Nur Taraki became leader of Afghanistan. He signed a Treaty of Friendship and Co-operation with the USSR. However, his government faced internal opposition from radical Islamic groups and a civil war broke out. In 1979, Taraki was replaced by Hafizullah Amin. But his government also struggled to control Afghanistan. So, in December 1979, the USSR sent in troops to hold the country under Soviet influence. On January 1, 1980, the pro-Soviet Babrak Karmal was made the new Afghan ruler. The invasion followed the Brezhnev Doctrine of 1968 (see p55).

WHAT IMPACT DID THE INVASION HAVE ON THE COLD WAR?

US-Soviet relations
The invasion brought détente to an end. US President Carter was furious. In 1980 the Olympic Games were to be held in Moscow. In January 1980 Carter announced a US boycott of the Games. Because the USA and USSR had two of the strongest teams, this badly damaged the Olympics as an international event.

More importantly, US Congress refused to **ratify** the SALT II Treaty (see p60). President Carter also stopped trade between the USA and USSR. This hurt the USSR because it now depended on American grain imports.

ratify
give support to

SOURCE 1

0   500 km

Caspian Sea

U S S R

CHINA

Tehran

Kabul
AFGHANISTAN   Islamabad

I R A N

P A K I S T A N   Delhi

Persian Gulf

N

OMAN   Arabian Sea

I N D I A

Afghanistan and Central Asia in 1979.

SOURCE 2 | US President Carter talks about the invasion in December 1979.

"This invasion is an extremely serious threat to peace. The invasion is a threat of further Soviet expansion into neighbouring countries of South West Asia."

**SOURCE 3** A cartoon from a British newspaper of December 1979. It shows President Carter watching the Soviet invasion of Afghanistan.

Carter and Central Asia

The Arabian Sea and Pakistan

Carter also sent a US naval task force to the Arabian Sea (see Source 1), where he feared the USSR was setting up a sea base. A Soviet sea base there would have threatened important international oil tanker routes in the Persian Gulf. Additionally, the USA began giving arms to Pakistan. Even though Pakistan was under a harsh dictatorship, the USA claimed it was defending the free world by arming it against the Soviet threat.

The USA and the Afghan Mujahidin

The USA also began training and arming the Muslim opponents of the pro-Soviet Afghan government. These Muslim groups were called Mujahidin ('fighter for Allah'). Several Mujahidin fighters came from other Islamic states. One came from Saudi Arabia: Osama bin Laden.

Carter's failure and replacement

Carter failed to stop the Soviet invasion. He also failed to get the US hostages released from Iran. In the 1980 presidential election he was defeated by Ronald Reagan.

WHY DID THE USSR LEAVE AFGHANISTAN IN 1989?

Guerilla tactics

Afghanistan proved to be the 'Soviet Vietnam'. The USSR had very advanced military equipment. Yet, with the backing of 125,000 Soviet troops, the Afghan government still couldn't control the country. This was because the Mujahidin used guerrilla warfare, like the Viet Cong. Although outgunned by the USSR, they used 'hit and run' tactics. Bridges and

tunnels were destroyed and military convoys ambushed. They also had a number of very effective weapons.

Afghan landscape and Soviet losses

The Mujahidin were aided by the geography of Afghanistan. It is a very mountainous country, providing many hiding places for the guerrillas. They could also attack Afghanistan from the mountains of Pakistan. Just like Vietnam, the Soviets lost thousands killed (20,000) and wounded. This made the war very unpopular within the USSR.

Gorbachev

In 1985 Mikhail Gorbachev became Soviet leader. He wanted to modernise the USSR and improve relations with the USA. In 1987 he started talks about a Soviet withdrawal. After signing an agreement in Geneva with US President Reagan in 1988, the USSR finally withdrew from Afghanistan in February 1989. The war in Afghanistan helped end communist rule in the USSR. But it devastated Afghanistan and created one of the world's worst refugee problems. Over three million Afghans fled. Many went to Pakistani refugee camps. When the USSR left, the pro-Soviet government fell. It was replaced by a radical Muslim government, led by the Mujahidin – or Taleban, as they were now called. This regime lasted until 2001. It was removed by US forces, following the terrorist attacks on New York on September 11, 2001.

Questions

1. Why did the USSR invade Afghanistan in December 1979?
2. Study Source 2. How useful is this source as evidence of US reaction to the Soviet invasion of Afghanistan?
3. Study Source 3. What statement is this cartoon trying to make about the impact of the Soviet invasion of Afghanistan on the Cold War?
4. How did the invasion of Afghanistan affect relations between the USA and the USSR? Explain your answer, using information and sources in this section.

Upheaval in Poland: Solidarity

In 1980 the focus of the Cold War moved back to Eastern Europe. In Poland a major effort was made to gain more freedom under communist rule. Not since the Prague Spring of 1968 had communist rule faced such a challenge.

WHY DID UNREST DEVELOP IN POLAND IN 1980?

Religion

Poland was a communist country, ally of the USSR, and a member of the Warsaw Pact. However, over 95 per cent of the population of Poland was Catholic. Under communism (which was atheistic) the Catholic Church was persecuted. As a result, many Poles wanted government reform. In 1978 a major change occurred in the Catholic Church. A Pole, Karol Wojtyla, Cardinal Archbishop of Krakow, was elected Pope John Paul II. This was the first time in 400 years that a non-Italian had become pope. This gave great hope for change to Catholics in Poland.

Bad relations with the USSR

Although Poland was 'liberated' by the Red Army in 1945, relations with the USSR had never been friendly. In 1945 eastern Poland was taken by the USSR. In return, Poland was given part of eastern Germany. Hundreds of thousands of Poles were forced to move. The whole Polish population of the city of Lvov was moved to the former German city of Breslau. It changed its name to Wroclaw.

The Katyn Wood discovery

During the Second World War, the Germans had uncovered the graves of thousands of Polish army officers at Katyn Wood in the USSR. The Poles believed that approximately 40,000 had been murdered by the Soviet secret police early in the war. The USSR had wanted to destroy the leadership of the Polish army. It caused great resentment in Poland.

Living conditions and freedom

Poor living conditions and lack of freedom helped cause unrest. In 1956 an anti-communist uprising took place in Poznan. This forced a change in government: Wladyslaw Gomulka became leader. But living conditions didn't improve much, and in 1970 more unrest developed. This time it began with shipyard riots in Gdansk, in northern Poland. Between December 16 and 17, 1970, armed police killed 45 demonstrators and wounded over 1,000 more. Gomulka was forced out of government. He was replaced by Edvard Gierek, who promised reform and better living conditions.

Debt, shortages, and strikes

In 1980 Poland was in economic crisis. It had one of the biggest debts in the world. It owed foreign banks millions of dollars. Between 1980 and 1981, the USSR had given Poland $3 billion to prevent economic collapse. To raise money, prices rose. There were food and fuel shortages. Again, there was trouble in the shipyard of Gdansk, where a strike broke out in August 1980. As the strike began, an unemployed electrician climbed over the fence into the shipyard. He was Lech Walesa (see Source 1). He became the leader of the strike. Strikes then spread all over Poland.

Lech Walesa and Solidarity

Walesa was a very good speaker. He got the strikers to act together. His aim was to create a

SOURCE 1

Lech Walesa speaking in 1981.

trade union movement free from Communist Party influence. The movement took the name Solidarity. Within months, Solidarity had a membership of nine million workers out of a total population of 32 million. It was a serious threat to communist influence in Poland and throughout Eastern Europe.

HOW DID THE POLISH GOVERNMENT DEAL WITH SOLIDARITY?

Negotiation

The first tactic was to negotiate with Solidarity and Walesa. He drew up a list of 21 demands. The strikers refused to leave the shipyard until the demands were met. Gierek's government fell. He was replaced by Kania. Eventually, an agreement was reached in November 1980.

What was in the agreement?

The strikers accepted that the Communist Party should dominate Polish politics, and that Poland should stay part of the Soviet bloc. In return, the government recognised the right of workers to strike. This was an amazing victory. No workers in communist-controlled Europe had this right. Even more sensational was the agreement to allow trade unions to be free from Communist Party control. Pensions and wages were increased, and promises were made to improve working conditions. A large monument to the 45 dead of December 1970 was to be erected in the Gdansk shipyard.

It seemed that a revolution had taken place. Almost overnight Lech Walesa became a name known throughout the world.

THE END OF SOLIDARITY

By 1981 economic conditions had not improved. If anything, they had become worse. In December 1981 strikes began again across Poland. A crisis was taking place. Kania's government fell, and an army officer, General Wojciech Jaruzelski, was appointed Prime Minister. The Soviet government told him: stop the strikes or face a Soviet invasion.

On December 12, 1981, Solidarity planned a national strike. Jaruzelski acted. He declared martial law. Solidarity

martial law
a period when army and police can arrest and imprison people without trial

leaders like Walesa were arrested. In the mining district of Upper Silesia, coalminers tried to resist by refusing to move from their mines. The riot police (ZOMO) used water to flood the mines, drowning the protestors. Jaruzelski had prevented a Soviet invasion, but at a very high cost.

> **SOURCE 2** General Jaruzelski's speech declaring martial law, December 1981. It was made live on Polish television.
>
> *"Citizens. It is my duty to take responsibility at this dramatic moment of Polish history. Poland's future is at stake."*

> **SOURCE 3** Lech Walesa speaking in 1995 about his arrest in 1981.
>
> *"In 1981 I said to the man who came to arrest me, 'This is the moment of your defeat. These are the last nails in the coffin of communism.'"*

After a year in detention, Lech Walesa was freed. However, he was not allowed to play a role in Solidarity. In 1983, he was awarded the Nobel Peace Prize. Solidarity weakened communist control of Poland. So did the election of a Polish Pope. In 1990, following the fall of communism in Eastern Europe in 1989, Lech Walesa was elected President of Poland.

INVESTIGATE...
Lech Walesa won the Nobel Peace Prize in 1983. Go to www.nobel.se/peace/laureates *and follow the links. Construct a timeline showing the key events of his life. Do you think he deserved the Prize?*

Questions

1. *Why had communist rule become unpopular in Poland by 1980? Explain your answer.*
2. *Study Source 2. How useful is this source as evidence of why martial law was introduced in Poland in December 1980?*
3. *Study Source 3. How reliable is this source as evidence about why communism had eventually collapsed in Poland by 1989?*
4. *Why was the Solidarity trade union movement such a threat to the USSR? Explain your answer, using information and sources in this section.*

Reagan: the man who won the Cold War?

WHO WAS RONALD REAGAN?

Ronald Reagan became President of the USA in January 1981. He was a Republican and had been a strong anti-communist all his adult life.

Reagan was unlike all previous US Presidents during the Cold War. From President Truman onwards, US leaders had tried to contain communism. Reagan was different. He wanted to win the Cold War. He believed that the USSR was an 'evil empire' that enslaved millions of people. He believed that the USA could defeat the USSR in the Cold War simply by acquiring more weapons. Because the USA had a stronger economy, the USSR would not be able to keep up. Sooner or later, the USSR would have to admit that the USA was the strongest superpower, or it would face massive economic problems.

SOURCE 1

Richard Perle, a top adviser to President Reagan, talking about the new American Cold War policy, which began in 1981.

"It was necessary to show that détente couldn't work in order to go beyond it. We aimed at victory in the Cold War."

HOW DID REAGAN PLAN TO MAKE THE USA SUPERIOR?

Increase defence spending

When he became President, Reagan ordered the biggest peacetime increase in US armed forces in history. Defence spending rose from $179 billion in 1981 to $370 billion in 1986. The Air Force acquired a new long distance bomber: the B1. Old battleships not used since the Second World War were returned to service. A new class of nuclear-powered aircraft carriers, the Nimitz, was built. New weapons were developed. The most spectacular were called Stealth aircraft, and were invisible to radar. They eventually saw service in the 1990s.

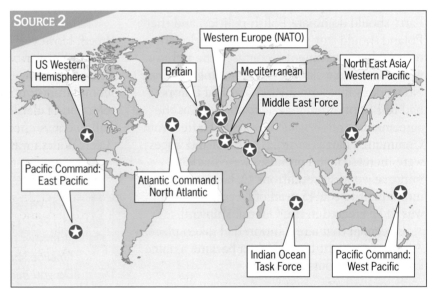

SOURCE 2

US Western Hemisphere · Britain · Western Europe (NATO) · Mediterranean · North East Asia/ Western Pacific · Middle East Force · Pacific Command: East Pacific · Atlantic Command: North Atlantic · Indian Ocean Task Force · Pacific Command: West Pacific

Worldwide US force deployments in 1987.

RONALD REAGAN (1911-)

40th President of the USA (1981-1989), Reagan was born in Illinois. From 1937 to 1957 he was an actor in Hollywood, appearing in 53 films. He became president of the Screen Actors' Guild, where he opposed communism in Hollywood. From 1966 to 1974 he was Governor of California. As Republican candidate in the 1980 presidential election, he was elected by a huge 489-40 electoral vote margin against President Carter. As President, Reagan survived an assassination attempt, and followed conservative policies. He greatly increased defence spending to try to win the Cold War, and cut taxes and welfare expenditure in the USA. He also supported anti-communist movements in Central America.

Weapons in Europe

New US missiles were deployed in Europe. In 1983 cruise missiles were placed in Britain. Pershing II missiles were placed in West Germany. Both types of missile were deployed to counter a new mobile Soviet missile, the SS20. Reagan was determined to prevent the USSR gaining an advantage in Europe.

Star Wars

Reagan announced his most controversial plan in 1983. It was called the Strategic Defence Initiative (SDI). It was also known as Star Wars. Reagan announced to the American people that he planned to make nuclear war obsolete. The USA was going to develop laser weapons to be deployed in space. These would detect and then shoot down any incoming Soviet nuclear missiles aimed at the USA.

WHAT WAS THE SOVIET REACTION TO REAGAN'S PLANS?

Andropov and START

In 1982 Soviet Premier Brezhnev died. He was replaced by Yuri Andropov, former head of the KGB. When he became leader, Andropov was already a very ill man. He was alarmed at Reagan's policies. In 1982 a new set of talks began between the USA and USSR in Geneva, Switzerland. These were called START (Strategic Arms Reduction Talks). For the first time, both sides talked about actively cutting their number of nuclear weapons. However, Andropov was very concerned about Reagan's Star Wars plan. The Soviets even considered a nuclear attack on the USA before Star Wars was properly developed. 1983 was the tensest year in the Cold War since the Cuban Missile crisis of 1962.

SOURCE 3 The historian Walter LaFeber, writing about Ronald Reagan in 1994.

'Many observers considered Reagan dangerous. He knew little about foreign policy, and seemed lazy and easily confused. The journalist Lou Cannon, who had followed Reagan since the 1960s, wrote that no one could remember when Reagan last read a book. "It's true hard work never killed anybody, but I think, why take a chance?" was one of Reagan's jokes.'

SOURCE 4 From *The Downing Street Years* by Margaret Thatcher, published in 1993. Thatcher was British Prime Minister from 1979 to 1990. She was a close friend of Reagan.

'It was easy for lesser men to underrate Ronald Reagan. He laid down general aims for his subordinates to follow. He was self-confident and good-natured. In addition to inspiring Americans, he went on to inspire people behind the Iron Curtain by speaking honest words about the evil empire that oppressed them.'

In 1984 the USSR and other European Communist countries refused to go to the Olympic Games in Los Angeles, USA. This showed how bad relations between the USA and USSR had become since the start of the new Cold War in 1979.

Gorbachev

After Andropov's death in 1984, another old, ill man (Konstantin Chernenko) was chosen to lead the USSR. He lasted only a year. Finally, in 1985, the USSR chose a younger, more dynamic leader: Mikhail Gorbachev. Unlike his predecessors, Gorbachev realised that the USSR could not compete with the USA in weapons production. Reagan had been proved right: the arms race had severely damaged the Soviet economy. Unless the number of weapons could be reduced, and the Soviet economy reformed, the USSR would collapse. The end of the Cold War was in sight.

Questions

1. What were President Reagan's aims in the Cold War?
2. Study Source 1. How useful is it as evidence to an historian writing about the Cold War in the 1980s?
3. Study Sources 3 and 4. These two sources give different views of President Reagan.
   a) In what ways do they differ?
   b) Why do you think they differ?
4. How did President Reagan try to gain US military superiority in the Cold War? Use information and sources in this section to support your answer.

Gorbachev: the man who ended the Cold War?

Mikhail Gorbachev was the last leader of the USSR. He ruled from 1985 to 1991. At 54, he was a relatively young leader for the USSR. His two predecessors were both old and very ill men. Gorbachev was an energetic leader, who became popular throughout the world.

MIKHAIL GORBACHEV (1931-)
General Secretary of the Communist Party from 1985 to 1991, and President of the USSR from 1989 to 1991. Gorbachev joined the Communist Party in 1952, and ascended the ladder of the local Party organisations quickly. In 1980 he became the youngest member of the Politburo (cabinet). During his leadership, he was famous for his policies of *perestroika* and *glasnost*, and for signing the INF treaty with the USA (see p69). He was awarded the Nobel Peace Prize in 1989.

WHAT DID GORBACHEV DO IN THE USSR?

The USSR was in a very poor economic position in 1985. Decades of very high defence spending had damaged the economy. Living standards were poor compared to the rest of Europe. Many government officials were corrupt. The USSR also had a high rate of alcoholism. In the 1980s the average life expectancy of Soviet men actually dropped because of this problem.

Perestroika and glasnost
Gorbachev wanted to make very radical changes. He introduced two new policies: *perestroika* and *glasnost*.
Perestroika
Perestroika is the Russian word for 'restructuring'. Goods made in the USSR were of a poor quality. Gorbachev wanted to improve both quality and output of goods by giving business and factories more control over what

they did. This meant less central control. However, less central control meant less control for the Communist Party.
Glasnost
Glasnost is the Russian word for 'openness'. Gorbachev wanted greater freedom for the media. Newspapers and TV were encouraged to criticise businesses and government officials that had done things wrong. This was a completely new experience for Soviet people.

How did these changes affect the USSR?
One of the side effects was the rapid growth in popularity of Western pop music. The young Soviets who enjoyed Western music also desired the same freedoms and standard of living as the West.

One of Gorbachev's most unpopular reforms was a tax on vodka. He encouraged people to drink soft drinks instead.

Unfortunately, Gorbachev's reforms were too little, too late. The USSR was in such a poor economic state that big changes could not occur. This meant that he became unpopular with old conservative communists, who disliked change. He was also unpopular with young radicals because change did not take place quickly enough.

HOW DID GORBACHEV AFFECT THE COLD WAR?

When Gorbachev became ruler of the USSR, the Cold War faced a big freeze. US President Reagan was intent on developing his Star Wars programme and new missiles were being placed in Europe by both the USA and USSR.

Geneva, November 1985
In November 1985, Gorbachev met Reagan in Geneva, Switzerland. This was the first time the leaders of the superpowers had met for six years. The most important topic was nuclear weapons. However, the two leaders could not agree on arms reduction. This was due mainly to Reagan's unwillingness to drop his Star Wars programme. Although the meeting did not lead to an agreement, at least both sides were talking.

Reykjavik, October 1986

The leaders met 11 months later in the capital of Iceland. At this conference Gorbachev put forward the Zero Option. This would mean Soviet withdrawal of all their SS20 missiles from Europe if the USA withdrew its Cruise and Pershing II missiles from Europe. After two days of intense talks no agreement was made, but one seemed close.

The Intermediate Nuclear Forces Treaty

Finally, in December 1987, both leaders signed the INF Treaty. This was the first nuclear arms reduction treaty in history. Both superpowers decided to withdraw their nuclear weapons from Europe, as well as destroying some. A further Nuclear Weapons Reduction Treaty was signed with Reagan's successor, George H. Bush, in 1989. This was the beginning of the end of the Cold War. Gorbachev had achieved the seemingly impossible.

SOURCE 1
The view of historian John Mason in *The Cold War 1945-1991*, published in 1996.

'Gorbachev came to power in March 1985. This marks the beginning of the end of the Cold War. Indeed, Gorbachev set out deliberately to end it.'

GORBACHEV AND THE COMMUNIST WORLD

China

In 1989 Gorbachev visited communist China. His visit inspired a great demonstration by young Chinese. The centre of the demonstration was Tiananmen Square in Beijing. They called for glasnost (openness) in China. Their demonstrations lasted until Gorbachev left China. When he left, the Chinese government sent troops to crush the

SOURCE 2
A Chinese student takes on government tanks in Tiananmen Square, 1989.

demonstrations (see Source 2). Thousands of young Chinese were killed. There was to be no new political freedom in China. However, like the USSR, the Chinese government reduced central control in the economy. Western companies were allowed to trade in China. A Kentucky Fried Chicken restaurant opened on Tiananmen Square with rice served instead of French fries.

Eastern Europe

In Eastern Europe things were much different. In March 1989 Gorbachev met the communist leaders of the region. He told them the Soviet army would no longer help them stay in power. This was the end of the Brezhnev Doctrine (see p55). The stage was set for a revolution across communist-controlled Europe.

Questions

1. In what ways did Gorbachev try to improve life within the USSR?
2. How did Gorbachev help to reduce the number of nuclear weapons in Europe?
3. 'Mikhail Gorbachev was the person responsible for making the end of the Cold War possible.' Do you agree with this statement? Explain your answer, using information and sources in this section.

Revolution in Eastern Europe, 1989

In January 1989, no one in Europe could have imagined the events that would unfold over the next 12 months. At that time, the communist governments of Eastern Europe had been in place for over 40 years. But, by January 1990 everything had changed. Every communist government in Eastern Europe had fallen from power. What is more remarkable was that this change took place with very little violence and bloodshed. Only in Romania was there serious fighting.

Why did this dramatic change take place?

THE ROLE OF GORBACHEV

Glasnost

Mikhail Gorbachev had made many changes within the USSR since he came to power in 1985. One of the most important changes was the policy of glasnost. This is the Russian word for openness. Gorbachev encouraged newspapers and TV to criticise any corruption or bad management. Instead of helping to strengthen communism, it weakened it. This encouraged people in communist Eastern Europe to criticise their governments.

The end of the Brezhnev Doctrine

The most important change made by Gorbachev came in March 1989. A meeting was held with the heads of all the communist governments of Eastern Europe. Gorbachev told them that the Soviet army would no longer help them stay in power. This was the end of the Brezhnev Doctrine. In 1956 in Hungary, and in 1968 in Czechoslovakia, Soviet troops had overthrown governments that had tried to make Western-style reforms. In 1981, the USSR had also threatened Poland with invasion if its communist government did not control the Solidarity movement. Now, in 1989, this had all come to an end. A big question remained. Was communism popular in Eastern Europe? Or was it only kept in power by Soviet military force? Time would tell.

> **SOURCE 1** Mikhail Gorbachev, talking about his meeting with the heads of the Eastern European communist governments in 1989.
>
> *"I told them that they were responsible for their own countries. 'You decide what reforms you need.'"*

THE FALL OF COMMUNISM

Poland

Following Gorbachev's announcement in March 1989, Soviet troops began to leave Hungary on April 25. Shortly afterwards, General Jaruzelski announced free elections in Poland. On June 4 the elections took place. Solidarity won a spectacular victory. In the upper house of parliament, the Senate, Solidarity won 99 out of 100 seats. In July, US President George H. Bush visited Poland and Hungary. This encouraged reformers to change government policy.

On August 24, communist rule came to an end in Poland. Tadeusz Mazowiecki became the first non-communist Prime Minister since 1946.

> **SOURCE 2** Lech Walesa, leader of the Solidarity movement in Poland, talking about the events of 1989.
>
> *"I knew the communist system was finished. The only problem was: what would be the best way to get rid of communism?"*

Hungary

On September 10, the beginning of the end occurred. The Hungarian government opened its borders with Austria. It allowed thousands of East Germans holidaying in Hungary to escape to the West. The Iron Curtain was cracking. Matters got worse for the East German government. On October 1, the Czechoslovakian and Polish governments allowed East Germans to enter the West German embassies in their countries. Several thousand more East Germans escaped to the West. The USSR did nothing.

The Wall comes tumbling down!

On October 18, East Germany's old communist leader, Erich Honecker, resigned. He was replaced by Egon Krenz. All East Germany was gripped with excitement. Would the new leader allow East Germans through the Berlin Wall? Large demonstrations occurred across East Germany. The breakthrough occurred on November 9, by complete accident. Gunter Schabowski of the East German government met journalists in East Berlin. The East German government had planned to allow East Germans to visit West Berlin on November 10. Without warning, Schabowski announced that border restrictions were lifted that very night. East German border guards did not know what to do. Thousands of East Berliners went to the Berlin Wall, and the guards opened the border. The Berlin Wall had been breached! By the end of 1990, it had almost been torn down completely.

SOURCE 3

People being helped on to the Berlin Wall, November 1989.

Czechoslovakia

Between November 17 and 27, the Velvet Revolution occurred in Czechoslovakia. Political prisoners were released. These included Vaclav Havel, one of the leaders of Charter 77 (see p55). By the end of the month, the communist government had fallen without a shot being fired.

Romania

The only serious fighting occurred in Romania. On December 21, an armed uprising took place against communist dictator Nicolae Ceausescu. Along with his wife, he was captured and executed by firing squad on Christmas Day.

By New Year's Day 1990, only the USSR existed of the old Soviet bloc countries in Europe. Communism had collapsed rapidly, and almost bloodlessly, because the Soviet army had not intervened.

SOURCE 4 A cartoon from the Guardian, a British newspaper, in January 1990. It shows the hammer and sickle crying. The hammer and sickle are symbols of communism.

Questions

1. Produce a timeline showing how communism collapsed in Eastern Europe in 1989.
2. Study Source 3. How useful is this source as evidence of the way ordinary people felt about the fall of communism in Eastern Europe in 1989?
3. Study Source 4. What statement is this cartoon trying to make about the events in communist Eastern Europe in the 12 months before it was drawn?
4. What do you think was the most important factor behind the collapse of communism in Eastern Europe? Explain your answer, using information and sources from this section.

Three days that destroyed the USSR

On August 18, 1991, Soviet leader Mikhail Gorbachev was on holiday on the Black Sea. That day he was arrested by Yuri Plekhanov – a top member of the KGB (Soviet secret police). This is how conservative communists in the Soviet government tried to seize power in the USSR. It started three days of revolutionary chaos. At the end of the three days, Gorbachev's career as leader was finished. So was the USSR. How did all this happen?

THE BREAK-UP OF THE USSR

By January 1990 all the communist governments of Eastern Europe had fallen. Now it was the Soviet Union's turn. The USSR was made up of 15 republics. By far the largest was the Russian Soviet Federative Soviet Republic (RSFSR). It covered 80 per cent of the country. In the west, Estonia, Latvia and Lithuania wanted to leave the USSR. They had been forced to join it in 1940. On March 11, 1990, the government of Lithuania announced its independence. The issue continued for a year. Then, on January 11 and 12, 1991, Gorbachev sent the Soviet Army into Vilnius, the capital, to occupy it. Fighting developed. Fourteen were killed, and hundreds wounded by the Soviet soldiers.

Something had to be done to stop the disintegration of the USSR. Gorbachev planned to produce a new Union Treaty between the 15 republics. He hoped this would end the desire for independence.

WHY WAS THERE OPPOSITION FROM CONSERVATIVE COMMUNISTS?

Gorbachev's policies
Many people in the Soviet Communist Party were very unhappy with Gorbachev. His policies had led to the collapse of communism in Eastern Europe. Also, his policies of perestroika (restructuring) and glasnost (openness) had made little change to life within the USSR. In December 1990 Edvard Schevardnadze, the Soviet Foreign Minister, resigned. He was one of Gorbachev's most important ministers and was upset about the collapse of the USSR's position as a superpower.

The Gulf War
On August 2, 1990, Iraq invaded Kuwait. Iraq was an ally of the USSR. In February-March 1991, the USA and its allies removed Iraq from Kuwait in Operation Desert Storm. The USSR did nothing.

Shrinking Soviet economy
In the first six months of 1991, the size of the Soviet economy shrank by ten per cent. Prices rose by 50 per cent in the same period. The economy was collapsing.

> **SOURCE 1**   Alexander Yakolev, an adviser to Mikhail Gorbachev, talking about life in the USSR under Gorbachev.
>
> *"We promised that things would get better, but things were getting worse and worse."*

The new Union Treaty
Gorbachev went ahead to produce a new Union Treaty. This would have made links between the 15 republics weaker. It would also give Gorbachev more power as President of the USSR. The conservative Communists felt they had to act to save the USSR.

BORIS YELTSIN

But Gorbachev's chief opponent within the USSR was not a conservative Communist. Boris Yeltsin was a radical Communist, who had been head of the Moscow Communist Party from 1985 to 1987. In 1987 he criticised Gorbachev for not making more reforms and was sacked. However, he made a comeback in 1989 and, in the first democratic elections in Russia since 1917, was elected President of the RSFSR in 1990. Gorbachev's greatest rival was now President of the largest republic in the USSR.

THREE DAYS THAT SHOOK THE USSR

August 18
Gorbachev was arrested by the KGB. This was on the orders of the Emergency Committee. This had been set up by conservative Communists. They replaced Gorbachev with his deputy, Gennady Yaneyev.

August 19

At 6.30am the 'Gang of Eight' (a group of eight high-ranking government and KGB members) told the Soviet people in a TV broadcast that Gorbachev was very ill and had to stand down as President. They also announced a ban on demonstrations and strikes. But they had already made a big mistake. They had not arrested Yeltsin, their most important rival for power. Following the TV announcement, tens of thousands of people in Moscow went onto the streets in protest. Many went to the Russian parliament building in central Moscow (the White House).

Yeltsin phoned Yaneyev. He said, "We do not accept your gang of bandits." Then, in front of the White House, in full view of the world's media, he climbed on top of a Soviet army tank sent to end the demonstrations (see Source 3). He called for an end to the attempted takeover of government. The crowds grew larger. The soldiers refused to stop them. The attempted takeover (coup) collapsed.

August 20

The Gang of Eight tried to regain control. They demanded that all people leave the streets of Moscow by the evening. These demands were ignored. Although three people were killed, Soviet tanks began to withdraw from Moscow. The coup was over. By August 21, Yeltsin was in control. He had Gorbachev flown back from the Crimea to Moscow. The Gang of Eight fled. One, Boris Pugo, shot himself rather than face arrest.

SOURCE 3

Boris Yeltsin, speaking on a Soviet tank in front of the Moscow parliament building on August 19, 1991.

| SOURCE 2 | Mikhail Gorbachev talking about why the coup of 1991 failed. |

"Everything we have achieved since 1985 has borne fruit. Our people have changed. It was this that stopped the coup from succeeding."

THE IMPACT OF THE COUP

By the end of August 1991, the rule of the Communist Party had been brought to an end within the USSR. Gorbachev issued a decree (law) ending the Communist Party organisation, closing its newspaper *Pravda* ('Truth'), and disbanding the KGB.

On December 21, 1991, the USSR ceased to exist. It was replaced by a new organisation called the Commonwealth of Independent States (CIS). Only 11 of the 15 republics joined. Latvia, Lithuania, Estonia and Belarus formed new states. On Christmas Day 1991, Gorbachev resigned as President of the USSR.

The USSR had disappeared. The Cold War was finally over.

Questions

1. Draw a time chart of the events leading to the collapse of the USSR.
2. Study Sources 1 and 2. These sources give different views of life in the USSR during Gorbachev's rule.
   a) Why do you think they are different?
   b) Which source do you regard as more reliable? Give reasons for your view.
3. Study Source 3. Does it fully explain why the Soviet coup of August 1991 failed? Explain your answer.
4. What do you regard as the most important reason for the collapse of the USSR? Explain your answer, using information and sources from this section.

Eastern Europe, 1968-89

In a GCSE History examination candidates are asked several types of questions. These include:

- The evaluation of sources
- The evaluation of sources using your own knowledge
- Writing extended answers using your own knowledge

A fourth type is the structured question. In this type of question candidates are asked to use only their own knowledge to write an answer. The answers are similar to extended writing answers but tend to be shorter.

QUESTIONS AND EMANA'S ANSWERS

(a) What happened during the 'Prague Spring' of 1968? *(4 marks)*

> In early 1968, the communist government of Czechoslovakia began to make reforms. The leader of the government was Alexander Dubcek. He wanted to create 'socialism with a human face'. This meant giving more rights to people. This included more freedom for the TV and press, which could now criticise the government if they wished. Businesses were also given more freedom. It seemed that there was going to be a new way of organising a communist country.

(b) Explain why the USSR got involved in Czechoslovakia in 1968. *(6 marks)*

> In August 1968, troops from the Warsaw Pact invaded Czechoslovakia. They were led by troops from the USSR. The USSR decided to invade because of the Brezhnev Doctrine. This was named after the Soviet leader of the time. The USSR believed that the reforms made by the Dubcek government would undermine communist government across Europe. They feared that Soviet influence within Eastern Europe would disappear. They even feared that the communist system within the USSR might be threatened. During 1968, Dubcek had been invited to the USSR to discuss his reforms. When he refused to change his ideas, the USSR felt it had no choice but to invade Czechoslovakia.

(c) 'The most important reason for the collapse of Soviet control in Eastern Europe in 1989 was the effect of 'Solidarity' in Poland.' Do you agree with this statement? Explain your answer. *(10 marks)*

> In 1980 a new trade union organisation was formed in Poland. It was called Solidarity. It had been created following the shipyard workers' strike in a shipyard in Gdansk. Its leader was Lech Walesa. The Solidarity movement spread all over Poland. The communist government agreed that it could legally exist, even though it was not organised by the Communist Party. However, in December 1981 the communist government introduced martial law. Solidarity was banned and Walesa was arrested. So, even though the Solidarity movement was important in 1980 and 1981 in Poland, it did not have much effect on events in communist Europe during the 1980s.
>
> There were other reasons for the collapse of Soviet control in Eastern Europe. The most important was the appointment of Gorbachev as Soviet leader in 1985. He faced a USSR close to economic collapse. To stop the collapse he introduced two policies, 'perestroika' and 'glasnost'. These meant 'restructuring' and 'openness'. However, neither policy could stop the economic collapse of the USSR.
>
> An even more important reason was Gorbachev's decision in 1989 not to support communist governments with the Red Army, as the Soviets had done in Czechoslovakia in 1968. So, in 1989, Hungary allowed people to cross to Austria, and the beginning of the end began. All across communist Europe, demonstrations took place. They wanted the end of communism. In Czechoslovakia the communist government fell without a fight. This was called the Velvet

Revolution. In Poland, free elections were won by Solidarity, which formed a non-communist government. In November 1989 the Berlin Wall came down and East and West Germany were united.

So there were many important reasons why Soviet control collapsed. The Solidarity movement was not the most important reason.

HOW TO SCORE FULL MARKS: WHAT THE EXAMINERS SAY

Question (a)

This question requires candidates to recall their own knowledge of a historical event, in this case the Prague Spring.

Emana provides several important sources of information about the Prague Spring. He identifies the leader of the Czechoslovak Communist Party. He can also identify the types of reforms that made this period of Czechoslovak history so important in the history of communist Europe.

As a result, Emana was awarded full marks: 4 out of 4.

Question (b)

This question requires candidates to use their own knowledge to identify reasons for a historical event, in this case the Soviet invasion of Czechoslovakia in 1968.

Emana again not only supplies reasons; he also explains them. He correctly identifies the Brezhnev Doctrine. Like its Western counterpart, the Truman Doctrine, this doctrine aimed to contain the development of Western-style ideas and government. Dubcek's Czechoslovakian government was seen by the Soviets as undermining Soviet and communist rule. Emana also points out that the USSR did give Dubcek an opportunity to moderate his reforms before the final decision was made to invade in August 1968.

As a result, Emana again scored highly, and was awarded 5 out of a possible 6 marks.

Question (c)

This question requires candidates to explain whether or not the Solidarity movement was the most important cause of the collapse of Soviet Control in Europe by 1989. Candidates will be expected to use their own knowledge to identify reasons for the collapse and to compare their importance with other reasons.

Emana structures his answer very effectively. He produces a 'for and against' style answer, directly linked to the issue in the question. First, he deals with the impact of Solidarity and explains, rather than describes, its limited role in undermining Soviet control. He then contrasts this with coverage of other factors, such as the economic collapse of the USSR.

A very important feature of Emana's answer is his ability to place factors in an order of priority. This clearly links directly to the question, which states that the Solidarity movement was the most important reason for the collapse of Soviet control. Emana also provides other, more important reasons.

This answer is an explanation that considers the relationships between a number of reasons. He directly addresses the issue of which was the most important. The quality of spelling, punctuation and grammar is good.

As a result, Emana was awarded full marks: 10 out of 10.

EXTENSION WORK

How similar were events in Hungary in 1956 and events in Czechoslovakia in 1986? Explain your answer, **using information and sources from the last chapter**.

(15 marks)

• OCR accepts no responsibility whatsoever for the accuracy or method of working in the answers given.

The Cold War and détente

In all of the major examination boards, students will be expected to engage in extended writing – i.e. writing essays. Essay questions usually carry the highest marks on the examination paper. **Remember: it is the quality of your answer more** **than the quantity of material you produce that is important.** When answering essay-type questions, refer to the Study Skills section on extended writing at the beginning of this book.

QUESTIONS AND KATE'S ANSWERS

(a) Why was there such a major crisis between the superpowers over Cuba in 1962?   *(10 marks)*

In October 1962, the most important crisis in the Cold War took place. It began when the USA found out that the USSR had placed Intermediate Range missiles on Cuba. The USA was able to find these by using U2 spy planes. The planes photographed missile sites across Cuba. The crisis took place because the USA was now within easy range of Soviet missiles on Cuba. Cuba was only 70 miles from Florida. Nearly all the USA was within range of these missiles. The USA was already threatened by missiles based within the USSR. However, they had at least a 15-minute warning of incoming missiles. They didn't have such a long warning period from missiles based in Cuba.

The USA was also very upset because it regarded all the Americas as their area of influence. The USSR now had bases on Cuba that threatened this area. If the USA allowed this to happen, they would appear weak and humiliated to all the Central and South American countries.

What made the crisis very serious was the way US President Kennedy reacted. He threatened nuclear war if the Soviets did not remove their missiles. That is why the crisis was so important.

(b) In what ways did relations between the USA and the USSR change between the years 1979 and 1990? You may use the following information to help you with your answer.

- 1979 Invasion of Afghanistan
- 1980 USA threatens to develop 'Star Wars'
- Reagan and Gorbachev
- 1986 INF Treaty signed

(15 marks)

In 1979 the USA and USSR were following a policy of détente. This means the reduction of tension. Since the early 1970s, the USA and USSR had agreed to limit the number of nuclear weapons they had. This took place in the SALT treaty of 1972. In 1978 the USA and USSR had negotiated the SALT II Treaty.

In 1979 relations became very bad when the USSR invaded Afghanistan. The USA reacted by boycotting the Moscow Olympic Games of 1980. Also in 1980, President Carter lost the election to Ronald Reagan. He was very anti-communist. He called the USSR the 'evil empire'. From 1981 he began to increase military spending in the USA.

In 1983 relations became worse when Reagan announced the SDI or Strategic Defence Initiative. This was also known as Star Wars. Reagan planned to put laser-guided satellites into space. This would stop Soviet nuclear missiles. It would end the idea of M.A.D., Mutually Assured Destruction. The USSR feared the USA might attack them with nuclear weapons without fearing attack from the USSR. By 1985, a new big freeze had taken place in the Cold War.

Relations improved after Gorbachev became Soviet leader in 1985. He wanted to lessen the tension in the Cold War. He wanted a return to détente. By 1986 he had negotiated the Intermediate Nuclear Forces Treaty with Reagan. Both sides decided to remove their Intermediate Nuclear forces from Europe. Reagan removed Cruise and Pershing II missiles. The USSR removed S4 and SS20 missiles. Even after Reagan retired as President in 1989, his successor George H. Bush carried on improving relations. Further nuclear weapons treaties were signed in 1989.

Finally, in 1989 a revolution took place in Eastern Europe. By the end of that year, all the communist governments had fallen across Europe outside the

USSR. Even the Berlin Wall had been demolished. This could only take place because Gorbachev refused to allow the Red Army to keep the communist governments in power.

So, between 1979 and 1990, relations changed considerably. From 1979 to 1985, relations became very bad. Détente seemed dead. Then, with Gorbachev as Soviet leader, relations improved. By 1990 the Cold War was over.

HOW TO SCORE FULL MARKS: WHAT THE EXAMINERS SAY

Question (a)

This question requires candidates to use their own knowledge to describe and explain an historical event, in this case why the Cuban Missile crisis was so serious. In doing so, candidates are expected to identify a number of different reasons.

Kate identifies several reasons why the crisis was so serious. Cuba was merely 70 miles from Cuba, and nearly all the USA was vulnerable to attack by Soviet missiles placed there. However, she doesn't mention that the Soviets were only able to place missiles in Cuba following Castro's Cuban Revolution of 1959. Castro, by 1962, had become a communist. The USA faced the problem of a communist country within the Americas for the first and only time. This made the crisis very serious.

Kate also mentions how the US response made the crisis serious. However, she could have mentioned that Kennedy decided to blockade Cuba rather than attack it. If he had attacked Cuba, it could have led to a Third World War. Kate's style of writing is good, and her argument is clear. Spelling, punctuation and grammar are of a high standard.

As a result, Kate was awarded 7 out of a possible 10 marks. If she had included the other reasons, mentioned above, and made links between reasons, she would have been awarded full marks.

Question (b

This question, like Question (a), requires candidates to identify reasons for an historical event, in this case the development of the Cold War during the 1980s. To identify causes, candidates will have to use their own knowledge.

Kate uses the guide information provided in the question very effectively. She is able to identify how events from 1979 to 1983, in particular, led to a major deterioration in US-Soviet relations. Not only does she mention the guide issues in the question but she goes on to explain their role. This is particularly true with 'Star Wars', but less so with the invasion of Afghanistan. To aid the development of her argument, Kate mentions the state of relations from 1972 to 1979, which strongly suggests that détente had been working. Also, Kate provides a definition of détente, which strengthens the quality of her answer.

Kate highlights the role of Gorbachev in bringing about not only a return of détente, but the end of the Cold War. She is able to identify a theme within the period of the 1980s. Before Gorbachev, relations were very poor. After 1985 they improved considerably. She is able to mention the importance of the INF treaty. Finally, the essay ends with an overall assessment in a conclusion.

The level of Kate's spelling, punctuation and grammar is high. The quality of her answer is enhanced by its division into separate paragraphs.

Kate's answer has a clear structure, reference to, and linking of, causes, and direct reference to all the events in the guide. As a result, she was awarded full marks: 15 out of 15.

EXTENSION WORK

'The work of Mikhail Gorbachev was the most important factor behind the end of the Cold War.' Do you agree with this statement? Explain your answer, **using information and sources from the last chapter**.

(15 marks)

• Edexcel accepts no responsibility whatsoever for the accuracy or method of working in the answers given.

ACKNOWLEDGEMENTS

Every effort has been made to contact holders of copyright material, but if any have been inadvertently overlooked the publishers will be pleased to make the necessary arrangements at the first opportunity.

The author and publishers gratefully acknowledge the use of examination questions from the Assessment and Qualifications Alliance (AQA) 36-7, 52-3.

The publishers would like to thank the following for permission to reproduce pictures on these pages.

(T=Top, B=Bottom, L=Left, R=Right, C=Centre)

The Art Archive 15; Salt talks, cartoon by Ronan R.Lurie, cartoonnews.com 60; They still want us to lose a little face, namely his... cartoon by Draper Hill/ The Commercial Appeal, Memphis, TN, used with permission 51; ©Corbis 24b, 32, Corbis/©Bettmann 10, 33T, 41, 42, 45, 46, 64, Corbis/©Bryn Colton/Assignments Photographers 68, Corbis/©Hulton-Deutsch Collection 30B, Corbis/©Wally McNamee 66; O.K. Mr President, let's talk, cartoon by Leslie Illingworth, Daily Mail 29/10/62/ photo Centre for the Study of Cartoon and Caricature, University of Kent 35; It's going to be a long week... cartoon by Mike Peters/Dayton Daily News 59; The Soviet invasion of Afghanistan – a grave threat to détente, cartoon ©Les Gibbard 63; Cartoon ©Andrzej Krauze 71R; Cuban fiasco, cartoon by Roy Braxton Justus, reprinted with permission, Minneapolis Star Tribune 33B; Novosti (London) 24T; Popperfoto.com 29, 34, 43, 48, 52, 55T, 58, 69, 73, Popperfoto.com/Reuters 71L; The Bird Watcher, cartoon by A.E. Shepard ©Punch Ltd 17L; Robert Hunt Library 17R, 27T & B, 31.

Cover picture: Atomic Bomb Explosion, Sub-Surface Blast, by Charles Bittinger, Oil on canvas, 1946, Gift of Martha Burroughs, The Naval Historical Foundation, Washington.

Index